LEADERSHIP
LESSONS
OF
JESUS

TIMELESS WISDOM FOR
LEADERS IN TODAY'S WORLD

Bob Briner & Ray Pritchard

GRAMERCY BOOKS
NEW YORK

This 2001 edition is published by Gramercy Books™, a division of
Random House Value Publishing, Inc., 280 Park Avenue, New York, NY 10017,
by arrangement with Broadman and Holman Publishers.

Gramercy Books™ and design are registered trademarks of
Random House Value Publishing, Inc.

Random House
New York • Toronto • London • Sydney • Auckland
http://www.randomhouse.com/

Printed and bound in the United States of America

[Previously published as two volumes: *The Leadership Lessons
of Jesus* and *More Leadership Lessons of Jesus*.]

Library of Congress Cataloging-in-Publication Data

Briner, Bob.
   Leadership lessons of Jesus : timeless wisdom for leaders in todays world / Bob Briner
and Ray Pritchard.
      p. cm.
   Originally published as 2 volumes: The leadership lessons of Jesus. Nashville ;
  Broadman & Holman, 1997; and More leadership lessons of Jesus. Nashville ; Broadman
  & Holman, 1998.
   ISBN 0-517-21922-0 (alk. Paper)
  1. Leadership—Religious aspects—Christianity. 2. Jesus Christ—Leadership. 3. Bible.
  N.T. Gospels—Devotional literature. I. Pritchard, Ray, 1952- II. Title.

  BV4597 .53.L43 B75 2001
  253—dc21

                                  2001033151

10 9 8 7 6 5 4 3 2

CONTENTS

THE
LEADERSHIP
LESSONS
OF
JESUS

This book is dedicated to our daughter, Lynn Briner,

who brings a special sparkle to our lives.

Your mother and I love you.

—Bob Briner

This book is gratefully dedicated to Andy Pritchard.

He is everything an older brother should be.

—Ray Pritchard

TABLE OF CONTENTS

ACKNOWLEDGMENTS

Dr. Ray Pritchard, the senior pastor of Calvary Memorial Church in Oak Park, Illinois, has been a great help with each of the previous books I have written. With *The Leadership Lessons of Jesus*, he has honored me by becoming a full partner in writing, a coauthor in every sense of the word. Pastor Ray, as I respectfully call him, has my deepest thanks for his essential contributions to this book.

I also want to thank Matt Jacobson, our editor at Broadman and Holman, who saw the importance of this book and has been a great source of encouragement; Bucky Rosenbaum, the editorial director at Broadman and Holman; and all the others at this great Christian publishing house who have worked on the many aspects of bringing this book to readers. You have my gratitude.

Our literary agent, Jeff Fink, worked hard with Matt Jacobson on the necessary business aspects of the book and is appreciated, as are Mary Ann Van Meter, my long-time assistant, and Jill VanHyning, who typed and retyped the manuscript.

My wife, Marty, like wives of all writers, puts up with a lot. I want to thank her for being both patient and helpful as this book came into being.

Finally, I have sensed the presence and help of the Holy Spirit more than ever before as I have worked on *The*

Leadership Lessons of Jesus. I give thanks with a grateful heart.

Bob Briner
Greenville College
Greenville, Illinois

Many people have helped make this book a reality. I am especially grateful to Mia Gale and Kathy Duggins, who keep my life organized on a daily basis so I can be free to do the things I do best. Cliff Raad has been a continual inspiration and my number-one supporter; he has an amazing ability to turn dreams into reality. I am also thankful for my friendship with Gary Olson, who models for me what this book is all about. Finally, I wish to thank my wife, Marlene, and my three boys, Josh, Mark, and Nick. They give me hope for the future while keeping my feet planted on the ground.

Ray Pritchard

INTRODUCTION

Who is the greatest leader in history? Of all the names that might be given in response to that question, one name stands out above the rest.

Jesus Christ.

From His birth in a Bethlehem stable to His death on a cross, He lived on this earth for less than forty years, leaving behind only a few hundred followers upon His return to heaven. He never wrote a book, taught a seminar, or created a detailed outline for His disciples to follow. After His departure, He sent the Holy Spirit to aid them in recalling what He did and said.

A few years later, His movement had swelled to include thousands of new believers. Soon His followers fanned out across the Roman Empire, spreading the good news He had taught them. Within five generations, the number of Christians reached into the millions.

Two thousand years have passed since He was here, yet His followers today number more than one billion, with millions more joining every year. The organization He founded—the Church—has branches in every country on earth.

Yet, ironically, His public ministry lasted less than four years. With no formal training and in the face of murderous opposition, He inspired such loyalty that His followers were willing to die for Him.

How did He do it? What principles did He follow? And do those same principles still work today?

The plan is quite simple. The Gospel of Mark is the basis for study, both because it is the shortest of the Gospels and because it is preeminently the "Gospel of action." As you read these chapters, you'll be journeying through the earthly life of Jesus Christ as witnessed by His friends and enemies.

If you have dismissed Jesus as irrelevant to modern life, brace yourself. Most of us know that Jesus was a great teacher and the Redeemer of the human race, but many people have never considered Him to be the ultimate leader. Who else has ever had His enduring impact? Human leaders come and go, but the legacy of Jesus has grown greater with the passing of each century.

Our goal in writing this book is threefold: First, we want to lay bare those leadership principles that made Jesus so incredibly effective. Second, we hope you will discover Jesus in a new and more personal way. Third, we want you to see how relevant the Bible is to the challenges you face every day.

We believe the principles Jesus embodied are applicable in any area, whether an office, a school, a small business, a multinational corporation, or a volunteer organization. This book is a team effort. Bob Briner works in the field of professional sports management and broadcasting; Ray Pritchard pastors a church in Oak Park, Illinois. Although the book is written from Bob's perspective (to make the reading easier), both have contributed to this project.

That's enough background. Now let's step back two thousand years to the dusty banks of the Jordan River where a man named John the Baptist addresses a huge audience. Listen as the world's greatest spokesman announces the coming of the world's greatest leader.

CHAPTER 1

WHO SPEAKS FOR YOU?

And this was his message: "After me will come one

more powerful than I, the thongs of whose sandals

I am not worthy to stoop down and untie."

Mark 1:7

Who speaks for you? Who talks about you? What do they say?

These are vital questions for every leader and every *potential* leader to ask continually, both of himself and of the quality of his leadership. What are others saying—to you, for you, and about you? It is safe to assume that if no one is helping communicate the message of your leadership, then no one is following you.

If a distorted message is being disseminated, the quality and precision of your communication need attention.

What others were saying was important to Jesus. The powerful and fascinating account of John the Baptist underscores this. John, perhaps the most effective advance man of all time, sets a high standard for leaders to follow when choosing a spokesperson, one that should be upheld by both leaders and those who speak for them (which is itself a path to leadership).

Despite John's tremendous success in paving the way for Jesus and His ministry, he was—in many respects—a strange choice by God the Father for a spokesman. He lived in the desert, wore odd clothing, and ate unusual food. But his oddity undoubtedly served to highlight his message. He wasn't like his audience *or* Jesus. The person most qualified to speak for you may be someone completely different from you who can nonetheless "tell it like it is."

The relationship between Jesus and John the Baptist demonstrates that truth is always the first and most important element of the spokesperson's message and that a quality spokesperson continues to speak the truth even in tough times when the truth may be unpopular. John the Baptist had powerful enemies, but he never cowered in the face of opposition. Today's leaders need to engender this kind of commitment in those chosen to speak for them. Jesus demonstrates a powerful way to do this; He appreciated John and highly honored him in public. If you are blessed with a loyal, quality spokesperson, don't hesitate to make your appreciation public knowledge—often.

In turn, John shows how to avoid a problem that besets many spokespersons. Far too often, I see spokespersons begin to think more highly of them-selves than of the people or messages they represent. Status, standing, and perks become more important than what or who they represent, ultimately damaging the enterprise. This did not happen with John the Bap-tist, who continually proclaimed that Jesus was greater than he. His famous statement in John 3:30 should become the motto for all public relations people: "He must increase, but I must decrease."

Jesus was interested in what others were saying. Later in His ministry, in what may be an early exam-ple of public opinion sampling, Jesus asked His disci-ples, "Who do people say that the Son of Man is?" He followed this with an even more important question, "But who do you say that I am?"

Leaders need to ensure that followers help to disseminate their message, thus extending the reach of their leadership. Leaders need to ensure that those speaking for them are both truthful and loyal. From time to time a leader needs to assess the way his public—whomever they might be—perceives him. Most importantly, a leader must confirm that those closest to him understand who he is and what he hopes to achieve.

CHAPTER 2

A CALL TO LEADERSHIP

And a voice came from heaven:

"You are my Son, whom I love;

with you I am well pleased."

Mark 1:11

The idea of a "calling," particularly for those not employed in some sort of professional ministry, is often seen as archaic, impractical, or quaint, even by Christians.

This view is damaging, both to God's kingdom and to individual lives and careers. As Christians, we must understand that God has a call on our *entire* lives, including our careers. To see this any differently denies both allegiance to God as our Creator and an understanding of the unbelievable price Jesus paid for us on the cross. It keeps us from living fully integrated lives in which all things work in synergy for our good and for the building of God's kingdom (for more on this, see *The Road Best Traveled: Knowing God's Will for Life* by Ray Pritchard [Crossway, 1995]).

Evidently, Jesus' leadership status needed to be reaffirmed by God the Father as Jesus began His earthly ministry; the voice from heaven saying, "Thou art my beloved Son; with thee I am well pleased" (Mark 1:11) was this affirmation. God has specific plans for each one of us, and we must do our best to determine what they are and submit to them. When we fail to do this, less than God's best often transpires. For example, a very gifted teacher at a Christian college—one *called* to teach—was railroaded into the college presidency by well-meaning colleagues, resulting in trauma, hard feelings, and disappointment on all sides. Gifts in one area, such as leadership abilities, are not necessarily transferable.

While it is certainly worthwhile to seek advice from others, ultimately a calling is between you and God. In an incident famous among our circle of friends, one friend told another, "I have put out the fleece for you," referring to the familiar incident with Gideon as recorded in Judges 6:36 38, "and here is what you need to do." Wisely, our other friend responded, "Hey, thanks, but I will put out my own fleece."

Never let someone else determine God's will for your life. No one else can understand God's unique call on your life as clearly as you. So many wasted years trying in vain to please others when they would be far more productive living as God designed them to live. This doesn't mean we go off half-cocked or without advice, but in the end, as Romans 14 says, each one of us must face God individually.

When we consider taking positions of leadership, we need to put out our fleece and seek God's affirmation. We may not hear an audible voice from heaven, but we can know that we are acting within God's will for our lives.

CHAPTER 3

TEMPTATION IS A PART OF LEADERSHIP

MARK 1:12–13

At once the Spirit sent him

out into the desert, and he was in the desert

forty days, being tempted by Satan.

Mark 1:12

Martin Luther said there are three things necessary to create a successful minister of God: prayer, meditation, and temptation.

Aspiring leaders must realize that the more effective their leadership, the more they will be tempted. The greater the ability to lead, the more powerful the temptations will be. Paul said in 1 Corinthians 16:8,

"A wide door for effective service has opened to me, and there are many adversaries" (RSV). A principal adversary for leaders comes from within—the temptation to abuse their leadership. Satan knew this when he put the greatest possible temptations before Jesus.

You can be sure the evil one will come after you as you become a more effective leader. Knowledge of, and preparation for, temptation is imperative. If God is calling you to a position of leadership, know that there will be very powerful temptations.

While temptation may lead to sin, temptation itself is not sinful. Rather, temptation—if successfully resisted—can reveal God's presence in our lives. Just as when the Spirit led Jesus into the desert, God may allow us to face potentially sinful situations that may be difficult for us to resist precisely so that we might develop godly character necessary for success in life, both on earth and in His kingdom. This is not to say that we should seek temptation. If we are doing our jobs, temptation will find us. To successfully overcome it, we must keep our eyes on Jesus while viewing temptation as a part of God's will for our lives.

I know of no one who understands the temptations that accompany leadership more than Billy Graham.

From the beginning of his rise to leadership and prominence as a proclaimer of the gospel, God allowed Dr. Graham to understand and prepare for the inevitable temptations he would face. Because he was prepared, he began and is completing his ministry as a strong, well-respected leader. Unfortunately, this cannot be said of many leaders, even biblical leaders. They failed to understand the awesome power of temptation, which led to their ultimate downfall.

Let's look at Billy Graham's example. He understood the variety of temptations that would be the most powerful for him and his ministry—lust, wealth, power, and pride. Dr. Graham built safeguards into his life and ministry to protect against each of these. Even now, he says that sexual temptation could still be a problem for him. To combat this temptation, he continues to enforce a rule for his life that began in the earliest days of his ministry—never be alone with a woman other than his wife. Some snicker at this, considering it overly cautious, even silly. Not me. I see so many Christian leaders (both in business and the church) who have fallen because of sexual temptation—their effectiveness as leaders destroyed, not to mention their witness and personal relationships. In my own business life, I never travel with my secretary, even though she has worked for me for more than eleven years. Many men I know routinely take their female coworkers or secretaries on business trips in the name of accomplishing their work more efficiently, but Billy Graham's example is good enough for me.

Greater access to wealth almost always accompanies positions of greater leadership. Some leaders are not able to handle this and have fallen as a result, either succumbing to the temptation to take more than was legally theirs or letting the pursuit of wealth dominate their lives. In God's eyes both of these are wrong, and both destroy leadership effectiveness.

Billy Graham wisely insisted that his evangelistic organization adopt the most stringent financial guidelines and that his own salary be set by a board of directors. Through the years his salary has always been extremely modest by most standards, helping to ensure that money did not dissipate the effectiveness of his leadership. The same board of directors that sets his salary helps Graham keep the attraction of power in check. He leads the board, but they have the final say in matters that effect the organization.

For many leaders, pride—a close relative of power—is the greatest of all leadership temptations. Looking good becomes more important than doing good. Leadership becomes the focus of the leader rather than the welfare of the organization and its people. Many American politicians fall prey to this temptation; "How will this play in Peoria?" becomes the operative question rather than "Is this the best for the country?" Although politicians are the most visible of those who succumb to the temptation of pride, no leader is immune.

Accountability is the best antidote for pride. Billy Graham understands this, and is always careful to keep a close circle of friends to whom he is accountable. He also credits his wife, Ruth, for help in this regard. I can relate to this. My own wife is quick to let me know when I begin to get "too big for my britches." Leaders need to be held accountable. A friend or group of friends who will tell you the truth and help keep pride in check is a must for sustaining godly leadership over time. By understanding and practicing this, Billy Graham has been an effective leader for more than fifty years.

In the words of the old hymn, "Yield not to temptation, for yielding is sin; each victory will help you some other to win." No man or woman can rise to leadership who has not experienced the truth of those words to some degree. Temptation comes with leadership. Understand this, and take instructions from Billy Graham's example—prepare for it.

CHAPTER 4

LEADERS CALL FOLLOWERS
MARK 1:14–20

"Come, follow me," Jesus said,

"and I will make you fishers of men."

Mark 1:17

The difference between management and leadership is chiefly in the way those being managed or led are motivated.

In most relationships there are elements of both management and leadership involved. In a pure sense, however, those being managed are usually compensated in some way for their services, and systems and techniques play a large role. On the other hand, pure leadership is characterized primarily by the way followers are motivated to please their leader voluntarily, and the leader typically possesses a more spontaneous personal style.

Jesus was both the greatest manager and the greatest leader of all time, and both His management skills and leadership abilities should be prized and emulated (see *The Management Methods of Jesus* by Bob Briner [Thomas Nelson, 1996]). In Mark 1:14–20, Jesus provides some of the most basic, yet striking and powerful, leadership lessons.

In some ways His earthly leadership began when He called His first followers—Peter (Simon), Andrew, James, and John—from which the most important lesson to learn is that He *called*. He asked. He didn't just walk by, expecting some sort of supernatural attraction to occur. He called. He asked those four, who were to become some of His most devoted and productive followers, to "follow Me . . . ," a "must learn" lesson for today's leaders.

When you feel called to lead, and when you discover someone you really want and need to be involved in your endeavor, don't be coy. Follow the example of Jesus and *ask* them to join you. People want to be asked and feel needed. Even when they say no—and some will—they will feel good about themselves and about you simply because you asked.

For some leaders, there will be times when people will ask to join them in their enterprises. This is fine, but don't wait for this to happen, particularly where key people are concerned. If you feel called to lead, whether in an initiative in your church, a civic undertaking, or a business effort, and you see your own Peter, Andrew, James, or John, step up and ask them to join you, to "follow" you.

Jesus called His disciples personally. When inviting a key person to join you, resist the strong temptation to extend your invitation through a third party or some impersonal means—a letter, fax, or phone call. Perhaps fearing rejection or embarrassment, some leaders are reluctant to contact potential followers face-to-face, a true leadership mistake. Real leaders rise to the challenge of personally inviting to the team those persons necessary for the greatest success. No other invitations have the power and appeal of the one-on-one method. Jesus *asked* people to follow Him, and so should you.

Jesus called His disciples to a person before He called them to the enterprise. I once received that kind of personal call and have never forgotten it. When the National Football League was just beginning to come into its own as a major professional sports attraction and new franchises were being added yearly, I received my call. Dave Dixon, one of America's greatest sports entrepreneurs and conceptualizers, called me from athletic administration at a small college.

Almost thirty years later, I remember the important part of that call verbatim. Dave said, "Bob, one of these days I am going to get a pro football franchise, and when I do, I want you with me." Wow! *That* is a leadership call. Some years later, Dave had his franchise, and I joined him in it, later joining him again in two other daring and innovative sports undertakings; his personal call was that strong. Even though I have basically retired from professional sports, I am not sure I could resist a Dave Dixon call declaring, "Bob, I want you with me." There is power in a personal call.

The current conventional wisdom relative to recruiting new business and professional personnel calls for focusing narrowly on graduates of the most prestigious universities. An MBA from Harvard is perhaps the ultimate credential for positioning on the fast track to a successful business career. This same way of thinking also dominates the church. Depending on the denomination, only those from a few select seminaries are seriously considered for prime ministry opportunities.

This was not the way of Jesus, although He surely would have considered the Harvard MBA of His day or the top seminary graduate; after all, He chose Paul—one of the best-educated men of his time—and Matthew—skilled in the business of his day. Jesus' example in recruiting effective followers suggests that we cast the widest possible net. Consider everyone on his or her merit. Accept talent, character, and commitment where you find it. Do your best to look beyond the surface of family background, social status, degrees, and the patina of appearance. Real leaders look hard for real people with real virtues. Jesus showed how spectacularly successful a leader can be with carefully chosen followers from all walks of life.

As you lead and call followers, don't fall into the trap of observing the conventional wisdom. Be sure you don't miss the most capable potential followers because you are afraid to go against the narrow focus of the world. Anyone can hire the best-dressed person with the highest class rank from the most prestigious college, even "bean counters."

Whether your vision for leadership involves leading a godly family, leading a Sunday school class, developing a new product, revitalizing a lackluster ministry, or starting a new business, be sure you speak about it with fervor, frankness, and faith. Those you personally call to follow must be infected with your enthusiasm for the vision.

Go back to the Gospels. You will see that Jesus laid the foundation for His vision when He promised, "I will make you fishers of men." But that was only the beginning. Jesus carried His vision through His death and resurrection. Remember from John 21 that Jesus' final discussion with His disciples took place during a *fishing* trip on the Sea of Galilee. Jesus never strayed from His initial vision, using the same motif He employed in His original call to challenge His men one last time.

CHAPTER 5

LEADERS TEACH WITH AUTHORITY

MARK 1:21–28

The people were amazed at his teaching,

because he taught them as one who had authority,

not as the teachers of the law.

Mark 1:22

Jesus taught with authority. In His presence, evil was repelled.

In an earthly sense, Jesus could teach with authority because He knew the Scriptures; He knew what He was talking about. But it was not just His knowledge of the Word that made Jesus the ultimate teacher. The Pharisees knew every point of the Law. Because Jesus was Himself the Son of God, His every word was absolutely authoritative.

Evil spirits were uncomfortable in His presence not only because He taught with authority, but because He was the embodiment of His message. He was the very antithesis of evil, and they could not stand to be where He was.

Leaders are *always* teachers. To be an effective long-range leader, you must teach with authority. You must be *prepared*. You must know what you are talking about. Remember, Jesus prepared for more than thirty years.

Be prepared.

As important as it is to know what you are talking about, it is perhaps even more important to *be* what you are talking about. Jesus could drive out evil spirits not because of what He knew but because of who He was. A leader's words, as vitally important as they are, will only go so far and impact so many unless they truly represent the reality in his or her life. A leader's call for commitment, integrity, dedication, and sacrifice will never be honored unless she or he is committed, honest, dedicated, and willing to sacrifice. Effective, enduring leadership calls for both precept *and* example.

A leader who speaks of what he knows and lives what he speaks will attract willing followers; those unwilling to be led will be so uncomfortable that they will be *very* willing to get out of the way.

CHAPTER 6

A LEADER TAKES CARE OF HIS PEOPLE

MARK 1:29–34

So he went to her, took her hand

and helped her up. The fever left her

and she began to wait on them.

Mark 1:31

A leader takes care of his followers and those important to his followers.

Those you are leading can only be effective when their needs *and* the needs of their families are met; an effective leader understands this and is sensitive to it. Serve your followers *and* their families.

This may sound "soft" to some hard-driving, goal-oriented modern leaders, but it is truly the ultimate hard-nosed formula for success. By removing obstacles to their focus, you enable your followers to concentrate on their given tasks. As strange as it may seem, the surest way for a leader to succeed is to put others first, including the families of those he leads.

Note that Jesus did not instruct one of His followers to help the woman up so that He could heal her; Jesus went to her and helped her up. He became personally involved in solving the problem—a small detail for someone with such an important mission.

It could have been argued that Jesus didn't have the time, but no one could criticize Him for not taking the time. Through this simple action, He proves that, although it is always easier to say, "Take care of this for me," it is often better to say, "Let me take care of it myself." Just as the woman Jesus healed acknowledged His grace by attending to the needs of Jesus and His followers, so will your followers and their families remember and appreciate your personal touch.

CHAPTER 7

LEADERSHIP REQUIRES DISCIPLINE

MARK 1:35–39

Very early in the morning, while it was

still dark, Jesus got up, left the house

and went off to a solitary place, where he prayed.

Mark 1:35

A leader is disciplined. If you expect discipline among your followers and lack it in your own life, your followers will first lose respect and then grow to resent you.

Mark is very precise in this passage, saying, "Very early in the morning, while it was still dark." Jesus disciplined Himself in the wise use of time; He was

THE LEADERSHIP LESSONS OF JESUS

up and at 'em early. More importantly, however, He disciplined Himself to a time of prayer and solitude— prerequisites for Christians to succeed in any kind of leadership position.

Finding time for both is not an option but a *requirement*. A habit of prayer is perhaps more easily developed than a habit of solitude. Leaders can pray at a variety of times and in a variety of places, but solitude must be sought diligently.

Solitude does not come naturally or easily. Although the nature of a leader-follower relationship requires some degree of togetherness, a leader must discipline himself and his followers to establish time apart from the team. Mark says that when Simon and his companions found Jesus, they exclaimed, "Everyone is looking for you!" We would say, "Hey, what are you doing? Everyone needs you, and you are holed up in your office with the door closed."

The fact that you are needed affirms your leadership, but followers must understand the need for regular periods of solitude. Great leaders, from Abraham Lincoln to Winston Churchill to Thomas Edison, followed Jesus' example of setting aside quiet times alone. So should you.

Jesus' reply to Simon's exclamation is also quite instructive: "Let us go somewhere else—to the nearby villages—so I can preach there also. That is why I have come." Evidently Jesus was recharged and energized by the time of prayer and solitude, ready to move on and tackle the job ahead. Prayer and solitude do not cut into a leader's time or lessen his or her effectiveness; they add to and multiply that effectiveness.

Many of us have the wrong idea about prayer and solitude. We think that part of life is what you do while you're waiting to do something really important. In that sense, we view prayer as equivalent to a football team doing pregame warm-up drills. Everyone knows that the drills only get the team ready for the big game.

However, there is a real sense in which prayer isn't the pregame at all. Prayer is where the battles of life are won and lost. We see something like this in Jesus' life. Again and again He gets alone with His Father and pours out His heart in prayer. Everything else that happens—the miracles, the teaching ministry, His confrontations with enemies—flows directly from His time alone with God. After all, the only place where His sweat poured out like blood was in a garden alone with God; He never struggled when faced with His enemies. He won the battle alone before leading His followers in the victory parade.

Prayer and solitude were vital to Jesus' leadership, and they are also "musts" for us.

CHAPTER 8

LEADERS
CARE

MARK 1:40–42

Filled with compassion,

Jesus reached out his hand

and touched the man.

Mark 1:41

The hard-nosed, knock-the-walls-down, slash-and-burn, victory-at-any-price kind of leadership always has its proponents; this kind of leader is often lauded—for a while.

However, enduring leadership, the kind that makes a positive, long-range difference, is always characterized by compassion. A compassionate leader cares about people, both as individuals and as a group. A compassionate leader simultaneously seeks the greatest good for individuals, the group, and the mission—not an easy task. What may seem good for an individual may not be good for the group or the mission. A leader must exercise compassion in a thoughtful, prayerful way.

Jesus proved that a compassionate leader need not be soft, sacrificing the group or the mission to protect the feelings of one person. Too often, Christian organizations do this in the name of compassion. I have seen trustee boards of Christian colleges keep a president in office when common sense dictated he should go, simply because they did not want to hurt him or his family. This is not thoughtful, prayerful, compassionate, or realistic. Although the feelings of the president and his family were protected for a while, the college faculty, several generations of college students, and all the supporters of the college—as well as its mission for God's kingdom—suffered.

Compassionate leaders care deeply about the feelings of individuals affected by their decisions, and they seek to deliver painful decisions in the most humane and caring manner. However, the greatest good for the group and the mission must also be considered.

Jesus showed great compassion when confronted with suffering. However, He often sent people away sad (as in the case of the rich young ruler) and—to accomplish His all-important mission—led many into lives of suffering, even martyrdom. He promised to show the great apostle Paul "how much he must suffer for my name."

Showing compassion sometimes requires breaking the rules, often in ways followers don't understand. In Jesus' time, touching a man with leprosy violated Mosaic law; according to the Law, Jesus would be rendered ceremonially unclean, thus unable to pray at the temple. Jesus' desire to help a poor leper outweighed His obligation to the Law.

CHAPTER 9

LEADERSHIP
AND TIMING

MARK 1:43–45

Jesus sent him away at once

with a strong warning: "See that

you don't tell this to anyone."

Mark 1:43

When Jesus came, He not only invaded space, but also time. Time and timing were central to His methods and His message. Everything He did was timed to perfection; the Scripture says that He came in the "fullness of time"—that is, at the perfect time.

Quality leadership demands a sensitivity to time. When we make decisions and when we announce them are sometimes more important than the decisions themselves. Timing is *that* important. I've sometimes

delayed making and announcing raises and promotions so long that much of their morale-boosting effect
was lost, a crucial yet common mistake in timing.

Premature decisions and public statements can be
even more devastating. When the Chicago newspapers
announced that Dewey had defeated Truman for the
United States presidency before the final outcome
showed just the opposite, they became the laughing-
stock of journalists everywhere. "Never early, never
late, but always right on time" is an epithet any leader
would love to have.

Jesus knew that a premature announcement of His
miraculous power would impede His ministry, so He
admonished the newly cleansed leper to tell no one of
his amazing healing. It wasn't that Jesus didn't want
others to know of His power, but that He didn't want
to attract them for the wrong reasons. Scripture tells us
that the leper could not keep the good news to himself;
he began to tell everyone, causing Jesus to stay away
from the towns and cities.

The fact that the people still came to Him "from
everywhere" only proves that the attraction to Jesus
was so powerful that even bad timing could not derail
His mission. Our leadership undertakings are not that

certain to succeed. Work and plan so that time works *for* you, not against you.

CHAPTER 10

LEADERS SHOULD EXPECT THE UNEXPECTED
———— MARK 2:1–12 ————

When Jesus saw their faith,

he said to the paralytic,

"Son, your sins are forgiven."

Mark 2:5

Leaders lead, managers manage. Often one person will fill both roles in an organization. Mark 2:1–12 introduces us to four men who did something all leaders must do from time to time: respond in a positive fashion to unexpected situations.

A pure manager, when faced with a situation outside the system, is unsure of how to respond. A pure leader, on the other hand, revels in the unexpected and responds with innovative brilliance, as Jesus did when confronted with the paralytic, unexpectedly lowered from the roof in the middle of His discourse.

The four men who brought the paralytic to Jesus demonstrated both brilliant, spontaneous leadership *and* competent management. Many pure management-types would have been so discombobulated by such a novel interruption that they might have fled the scene. Not Jesus. His brilliance as a leader allowed Him to respond in a way that made good things happen. A leader turns the unexpected into advances for his cause.

No other leader, no matter how brilliant, will have the supernatural ability of Jesus to know what those around him are thinking. But a leader must have the ability to evaluate a situation on the spot, to get a feel for what is taking place, and to make the situation work for good.

My longtime friend and business partner, Donald Dell, is one of the all-time great negotiators, negotiating some of the most famous contracts in professional sports while representing such world-class athletes as Arthur Ashe and Michael Jordan. Much of this talent stems from his ability to discern what others are thinking and feeling. In a room filled with lawyers, accountants, and managers—often hostile and adversarial—Donald has the uncanny ability to sense their mood and tailor his responses accordingly. Our clients benefit enormously from this.

There in Capernaum, Jesus knew the thoughts of the people gathered in the house, particularly the thoughts of His adversaries. This knowledge, paired with His innate leadership ability, allowed Him to respond in a way that produced the greatest good. While much of this talent is inherent and God-given, it can certainly be developed and nurtured. Sometimes the talent is there, wasted by a lack of boldness. Many times I have understood a situation, known what I should say to accomplish the greatest good, but—ruled by timidity—I kept quiet. *Carpe diem*—seize the day—should be a key phrase for leaders.

Some people have the uncanny ability to be bold in negative ways or the propensity to say the wrong thing at the wrong time; they are the launchers of the proverbial "lead balloon." Because none of us is Jesus, this happens to all of us sometimes and should not deter us from developing and exercising leadership. However, Jesus was careful not to humiliate His opponents;

instead He challenged them to consider the ultimate questions of life. He could have said, "You dummies. Can't you see that I am God?" But He didn't. He threw a question in their faces that forced them to think deeply. By challenging the paralytic to "Rise and walk," He established proof of His authority; everyone was able to check the results for themselves. Either the man got up or He didn't. Jesus not only forgave the man, but also healed him so that His opponents might acknowledge who He was—no humiliation, just a question to ponder long after the miracle was over.

A leader knows the difference between leadership and management, and values both. He is ready to respond in positive ways to the unexpected, consistently analyzing situations and responding with boldness as he is led by the Holy Spirit.

CHAPTER 11

LEADERS ARE TEACHERS

A large crowd came to him,

and he began to teach them.

Mark 2:13

Leaders are teachers. No matter what the enterprise—a family, school, church, or business—leaders are teachers. The terms are not interchangeable; not all teachers are leaders, but all leaders *are* teachers.

Jesus was addressed as "Rabbi" or "Teacher" more often than any other title, primarily by His disciples and the multitudes He taught. When the crowds came to Him, He didn't organize a pep rally or whip the increasingly larger and larger crowds into a frenzy with self-aggrandizing, flashy rhetoric; that is the way of a demagogue, not a leader.

A leader uses charismatic appeal, not only to evoke emotions but also, much more importantly, to teach. The power and cogency of the lessons are equally as important as the emotions stirred. In leadership, reaching both the heart *and* the head are important.

Many people are surprised when they first hear Pastor Jim Cymbala preach. Because he is the senior pastor of the ten-thousand-member Brooklyn Tabernacle—home of the world-famous Brooklyn Tabernacle Choir, which produces some of Christendom's most soul-stirring music—many expect fiery, flashy, demonstrative preaching. There is certainly nothing bland about Pastor Cymbala's presentations, but he is first and foremost a teacher of God's Word, relying on the power of the message—not the attractiveness of the messenger—to move his listeners to repentance and obedience. He leads his great church by teaching.

In this passage from Mark, it is not a coincidence that the teaching of Jesus preceded His call to Matthew. When the crowds came, Jesus began to teach, even as He walked along. Matthew undoubtedly had heard Jesus teach before in Capernaum, His adopted hometown. No doubt Matthew was moved to follow Jesus because of His teachings, not to discount the amazing appeal of the person of Jesus; He attracted multitudes, but those who followed closely and continually were those He taught.

When Jesus spoke those life-changing, history-changing words to Matthew—"Follow me"—he obeyed because he was moved by both the beauty of the Master *and* the power of His teaching. A leader attracts people to a cause and holds them with the power of his or her teaching. Only lessons well learned and fully internalized hold followers for the long pull; it is only these lessons that keep followers faithful and committed when the inevitable tough times come.

CHAPTER 12

CHOOSING
A TEAM

"Follow me," Jesus told him,

and Levi got up and followed him.

Mark 2:14

My first jobs were coaching in high schools, long before I did anything but dream about the career in professional sports that came much later. An executive position with the Miami Dolphins may seem a long way from coaching at a small high school in the Flint Hills of Kansas, but—because the principles learned in those small schools were similar to those necessary for success in professional sports—it wasn't really that far.

As a high school coach, I learned that when you have no paid staff and depend entirely on volunteers, it is *very* important to choose those volunteers carefully. One key to a high school coach's success is the student manager. Get a good one—a fully committed one— and many of the logistics of running a high school sports team can be handled without your involvement. A smart manager can be a coach's eyes and ears among his players in a way that no one else can. A good student manager is vital to running a good program.

A wise old athletic director—one of my first bosses—told me never to choose the most attractive, outgoing, or popular candidate for the position of student manager, particularly not one popular with the girls. Rather, he recommended selecting the smart but shy, introverted kind who failed to stand out in any area. His theory was that this type of kid (who had almost no friends and no other claim to fame) would be so grateful to you for plucking him out of obscurity that he would work like a beaver with unfaltering loyalty.

This great advice provided my teams with a succession of super student managers. An important corollary is that these students, given a little attention and allowed to be on the edge of the spotlight, often blossomed into terrific student leaders in other areas. My old athletic director could well have learned his selection theory from Jesus.

In choosing Matthew, a despised tax collector, Jesus certainly went against conventional wisdom, looking far beneath the surface of Matthew's unpopular profession to teach us quite an important leadership lesson: a wise leader builds his or her team very carefully. Choices are made *not* on appearance and appeal but on deeply, prayerfully considered values. One of the selection criteria should be considering who will most appreciate being chosen. Jesus visited this theory again in the parable of the forgiven debt (Luke 7:41–43)—the one most forgiven loves the most.

By choosing Matthew, Jesus showed that a leader should consider diversity when building his team—*all* kinds of diversity, particularly diversity of talent, temperament, and experience. A less thoughtful leader puts together a homogeneous team of look-alikes who may also think alike because of their similar backgrounds and experiences—a much weaker team than one built with diversity in mind. We often think that diversity weakens a team when, in fact, the opposite is true. Men like Matthew and Peter (a tax collector and a fisherman, respectively) should have been at each other's throats—imagine a longshoreman having to work with an IRS agent. But Jesus saw something in these men and wasn't afraid to choose them both for the same team. Only a great leader would risk that; only an extraordinary leader could pull it off.

CHAPTER 13

EATING WITH
THE TROOPS

MARK 2:15

While Jesus was

having dinner at Levi's house . . . .

Mark 2:15

Leaders eat with their troops. Food can be a great catalyst for building relationships and for teaching.

It is not just coincidence that Scripture so often uses food as a metaphor for knowledge and learning; bread, meat, fish, milk, and honey are all biblical synonyms for knowledge. The Gospels reveal how often food and drink are the backdrops for so many of Jesus' most powerful and important lessons (e.g., the Last Supper). They are spread throughout the New Testament, from the miracle of turning water into wine to the poignant way Jesus appeared to His disciples after the Resurrection as He cooked their breakfast by the shore of the Sea of Galilee.

Leaders do not neglect the power that food and mealtimes have to set the stage for building lasting, productive relationships and imparting important lessons. Leaders never forget how easily their followers can be intimidated. Nothing breaks down barriers like sharing a Coke and a hamburger or a quick breakfast together.

Memos, manuals, and seminars are useful instructional tools, but they can never replace the quiet lunch or dinner as a means of teaching, learning, and growing together. Private executive dining rooms and solitary working lunches may have their place in a leader's life, but the wise leader will be sure to "break bread" occasionally with those he seeks to lead.

CHAPTER 14

FACING
OPPOSITION
———————MARK 2:15–17———————

"I have not come

to call the righteous, but sinners."

Mark 2:17

Leaders must be able to face opposition with equanimity and confidence. The ability to hold one's own when faced with criticism builds tremendous confidence in followers.

Imagine how thrilling it was for Matthew and the other disciples to hear Jesus, with punch and power, respond to the criticism of the Pharisees: "I have come not to call the righteous, but sinners [to repentance]." Matthew and his fellow citizens must have been cowed and beaten down often by the haughty, law-spouting Pharisees. In Jesus they had found a champion to challenge these self-righteous hypocrites. By silencing the snipers with His potent response, He strengthened and solidified His leadership position.

Teachers can teach best in congenial settings conducive to learning, while leaders can teach even in hostile settings when faced with powerful attacks. Like Jesus at Matthew's home, leaders are prepared for the inevitable challenges.

Leaders know what they are talking about. They understand their mission and how to articulate it. We live in the media age, in which sound bites often are called for. Leaders must have their sound bites ready to inspire prospective followers.

Certainly Jesus taught in very thoughtful, comprehensive ways, as in the Sermon on the Mount and through His powerful parables. But very often He taught with what today we call "sound bites"—pithy, potent, precise comments that stopped the debate. Jesus was the ultimate counterpuncher; His opponents struck the first verbal blow, but He always struck the last.

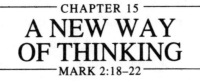

CHAPTER 15

A NEW WAY
OF THINKING

MARK 2:18–22

"And no one pours

new wine into old wineskins."

Mark 2:22

It is not enough to have a new way of doing things or a new way of thinking, even if your way is better.

Change that ignores context eventually leads to anarchy. Leadership requires an understanding of newness in the context of the old; to put it more simply, a leader must know what is going on. He or she must also be able to articulate why the new way is better.

Truly innovative leaders will always be challenged by those who protect the old ways of doing things. Upon a closer look, these are usually the same people who are protected by the way things have always been done. Change always threatens some people.

Jesus brought more change and profound newness to life than anyone else in the history of the world. As a result, He was challenged at every turn, but He met each challenge with beautifully thought-out and cogently articulated responses, many of which constitute some of the most famous quotes of all time.

Think about them:

- "Render therefore to Caesar the things that are Caesar's, and to God the things that are God's" (Matt. 22:21, RSV).
- "Let him who is without sin among you be the first to throw a stone" (John 8:7, RSV).
- "Get up, take your mat and walk" (Mark 2:9).
- "I will make you fishers of men" (Mark 1:17).
- "You are the salt of the earth" (Matt. 5:13).
- "Love your enemies" (Matt. 5:44).
- "Turn . . . the other cheek" (Matt. 5:39).
- "No one can serve two masters" (Matt. 6:24).
- "Do not throw your pearls before swine" (Matt. 7:6, RSV).
- "By their fruit you will recognize them" (Matt. 7:16).

Never fall into the trap of thinking that because something is inherently better it will automatically succeed. Competent, compelling leadership must be exercised to ensure that even the best things endure. Sony's Betamax was, by almost all accounts, the best video system and Apple's Macintosh the best personal computer, but Beta is long-gone and many experts say the same thing may happen to the Mac. The leaders of Sony and Apple were never able to position their superior products for lasting success. Leadership failed to articulate why their products were superior.

According to author Tom Peters, innovative companies do two things very well: (1) they remain true to their core values, and (2) they continue to evolve and change their methods of doing business. In his book *In Search of Excellence*, Peters notes that Proctor and Gamble has kept one brand of soap on the market for more than one hundred years and, in the process, has reformulated it more than *one hundred times!* Jesus never lost sight of His core values, and yet He continually evaluated the present context and adjusted accordingly. The change Christ brought always occurred within the context of the moment.

CHAPTER 16

LEADING WITH AND THROUGH TRADITIONS

MARK 2:23–28

Then he said to them,

"The Sabbath was made for man,

not man for the Sabbath."

Mark 2:27

A leader has respect for traditions, but he has a greater respect for people. If a tradition is valid and helpful, a leader will use the tradition to help accomplish his goal.

Jesus did this in many ways, using the traditions that glorified God to help people understand Him and His will. However, Jesus was careful to brush aside traditions that were onerous or nonsensical and did not reflect the nature of God. Discerning the difference is critical.

Some would-be leaders attract temporary followers by indiscriminately, often ostentatiously, denegrating tradition. There are those who are attracted to the iconoclast, but this is not the way of a true leader. A real leader understands that tradition can be good, often unifying and energizing. A wise leader values those traditions that are useful in making people better and in making things better for people.

But traditions that inflict unnecessary burdens on people should always be a target for the effective leader. "We have always done it this way" is not a validating concept for a leader; a quality leader instead asks "Why?" and "Can we do it better?" When convinced a new way is better, a leader immediately begins to establish a new tradition, one better than the old. A leader believes in the old saying, "He has the right to criticize who has the heart to help." Simply blasting an old tradition is not leadership.

When leaders must break tradition, however, they find a way to explain their new ideas in terms that followers can understand. By appealing to both the Scriptures and the account of David eating the consecrated bread, Jesus answered the Jews in terms they could understand. It's easy to say, "Out with the old, in with the new, and forget the past." But it is better to go "back to the future" by finding a precedent in the past for the changes you want to make in the present. Some leaders feel shackled by the past when they should see the past as an ally.

Tradition in and of itself is neither good nor bad. Wise leaders—especially those in established companies—must use the past but not be shackled by it. Tradition can sometimes become a chain if it keeps us from doing what needs to be done, which is what Jesus meant when he said, "The Sabbath was made for man, not man for the Sabbath."

Whether your area of leadership is in a home, school, church, civic organization, or business, how you handle the traditions there will help to determine how effective you are as a leader. A good _manager_ makes the existing system work to his or her advantage; a good _leader_ questions the system, making the changes necessary for improvement. In Jesus, the ultimate leader, old things have passed away and all things have become new.

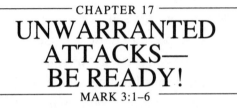

CHAPTER 17

UNWARRANTED ATTACKS— BE READY!

MARK 3:1–6

Then the Pharisees went out

and began to plot with the Herodians

how they might kill Jesus.

Mark 3:6

A wise leader understands that no matter how pure the motive or how effective the action, there will always be those who oppose his or her leadership.

A leader should not be surprised or debilitated by opposition because it *will* come. Those not ready for it are often so stunned that they abdicate or resign their leadership positions. Some are not temperamentally suited to handle opposition, which comes even in the face of pure motives and quality, effective action; these people are not suited to be leaders because they are unwilling to pay the emotional price required when attacked while doing good. This is OK. Not all are called to be leaders. In fact, this is a good test of leadership: can you handle unwarranted criticism? Many can cope with rational criticism, but only a select few can both understand and effectively deal with the kind of criticism that has no logical basis.

Arthur Ashe was a great tennis star known for his coolness under fire. He and I were close friends for more than twenty-five years. The only time I ever saw him lose his composure was when he was the subject of an unwarranted attack by the very people he was working so hard to help.

As the president of the Association of Tennis Professionals, Arthur worked hard and sacrificed a great deal to help the players who were not the great stars, those who often lost in the early rounds of tournaments. In spite of all logic, these players verbally attacked Arthur in a pre-Wimbledon players' meeting, and the injustice and irrationality of the criticism caused Arthur to explode. Never again did I see him put himself in a leadership position that would subject him to that kind of direct attack. He learned something about his ability to lead in the face of unwarranted opposition, a lesson all potential leaders need to learn.

Leaders will be criticized. Good, effective, benevolent leaders are often criticized most. Be ready!

CHAPTER 18

THE
INNER CORE

MARK 3:7–8

Jesus withdrew with his disciples

to the lake, and a large crowd

from Galilee followed.

Mark 3:7

Even those who lead masses of people must have a small inner core of followers who receive special attention; a leader who keeps everyone at arm's length never accomplishes the maximum.

I know a college president—a brilliant educator, administrator, and writer—who (despite his great personal charm) was never able to develop close relationships with members of his administrative teams.

Oddly, he seemed more at ease with crowds than in more intimate settings. He did fine work and represented his schools well. Although he accomplished a lot, he always seemed to move before he had completed his work and the most good could be accomplished. Insiders always cited a lack of close relationships with those he led as a reason for his shortened tenure.

Jesus made sure that concentrated attention was given to an inner circle of followers. Scripture tells us He spoke to the crowds but *taught* His disciples, saving some of the most important lessons for only three—Peter, James, and John. He often imparted more vital messages individually, as He did with His earthly brother James after the Resurrection, illustrating one of the most important and vital leadership lessons of Jesus: a very special, close relationship with a small group of followers is an *absolute essential* for the effective leader.

Concentrating exclusively on the masses rarely leaves a positive leadership legacy. A leader who imparts special insight and inspiration to a select few will have tremendous long-range results because those select few will continue to implement the leadership objectives in which they have come to believe. Consider the amazing results Jesus' disciples achieved *after* He left them.

There are certainly occasions when a leader needs to address the crowds. The effective leader works to develop skills, sensitivity, and comfort with crowds and small groups. While some are more naturally gifted in one setting than in others, it is possible to improve in both areas. If you aspire to be a leader (or perhaps a *better* leader), assess your strengths and weaknesses in each area and work to improve.

CHAPTER 19

LEADERS
PLAN

MARK 3:9

Because of the crowd he told

his disciples to have a small boat ready for him,

to keep the people from crowding him.

Mark 3:9

Leaders instantaneously react to unexpected opportunities and obstacles, enabling them to maximize unanticipated situations.

This does not mean they do not plan. Visionary leadership requires both a long-range view of opportunities and short-range plans to advance to the next level. Measure your leadership by this. Do you have the ultimate goal clearly in mind? Do you know how to move to the next step?

Details are important. A friend once asked Michelangelo why he had labored so long over the intricate details of the Sistine Chapel in Rome, details so tiny no one would ever notice.

"After all," the friend said, "who will know whether it is perfect or not?"

"I will," the artist replied.

The passage of time has fully vindicated Michelangelo's painstaking attention to detail. Hundreds of years later his matchless frescoes are regarded as among the greatest works of art ever produced.

Is God interested in the details? Read Exodus 25–40 and study God's extremely detailed instructions for the construction of the tabernacle. He provides a blueprint any architect would admire. God cares about the details and so should we.

Jesus dealt with admiring and hostile crowds throughout His ministry, always planning for them. Whether it was telling His disciples to prepare a small boat for Him so He could be apart from them or leading them to a mountainside so He could more effectively address them, He always had a plan that complemented His leadership style.

Jesus' master plan is the most brilliant and awe-inspiring one ever conceived. He repeatedly demonstrated His leadership abilities through the precision of His planning. In even the seemingly small things, He led by planning; from the colt ready for His triumphal entry into Jerusalem to an upper room ready for the Last Supper, He made things happen by planning.

Follow His perfect example. Be a leader.

Be a planner.

CHAPTER 20

STRATEGIC
WITHDRAWAL
MARK 3:8–12

But he gave them strict orders

not to tell who he was.

Mark 3:12

Strategic withdrawal is almost always a necessary part of success.

The wise leader knows that he will never go uninterrupted, undeterred from victory to victory; there will always be times when a thoughtful leader retreats: in baseball, the intentional walk; in football, the punt—sometimes even on third down; in all sports, the time-out to regroup. In every ongoing real-life situation there will be times when "discretion is the better part of valor," when a withdrawal, retreat, or time-out is not only necessary but *desirable*. The unwise leader can let ego, bravado, or wishful thinking make him or her forget that leadership in a worthwhile effort must take into account "the big picture." A lost battle or a strategic retreat in an overall winning effort is really a victory.

When the Pharisees plotted with the Herodians to kill Jesus after He healed the man's hand on the Sabbath, He could have confronted them on the spot. He could have taken a bold stand, but, in His wisdom, He didn't; He withdrew. When the evil spirits fell down before Him and cried out, "You are the Son of God," He could have said, "Yes. Go tell everyone." He didn't. He knew the time was not right; His troops were not ready. It was time for a third-down punt, so He gave strict orders for them not to reveal His true identity.

Sometimes you just have to yell, "Time-out!" If Michael Jordan needs a breather or Joe Montana needs to talk to the coach, we shouldn't feel badly about taking a break from the hectic routine to confer privately with our most trusted associates.

In both business and church life, I have seen worthwhile efforts end in futility because leaders were unwilling to strategically withdraw or take a tactical time-out, typically because of their excessive zeal or shortsightedness. In business, some executives invest so much ego in a plan, product, or program that they are unable to abandon a loser, even in the face of mounting losses and certain failure.

Some pastors and church leaders become so sure that their plans for evangelism, church growth, or a new building are on target that they insist on forging ahead in the face of congregational apathy or even outright opposition, unwilling to take a tactical time-out—to put things on hold—while they educate, encourage, and build a consensus. When this happens, churches are split, the plan—no matter how good—never materializes, and God's kingdom remains stagnant.

A wise leader picks his or her spots, retreating when necessary to accomplish the most good. Leadership often requires "taking one's lumps" and "biding one's time." Jesus demonstrated this leadership lesson for us so often and so brilliantly that it is one we should never forget.

CHAPTER 21

THE
PLACE

MARK 3:13

Jesus went up on a mountainside

and called to him those he wanted,

and they came to him.

Mark 3:13

Through Jesus' example we see that place is an important consideration. An effective leader chooses the most appropriate place to impact his or her important occasions.

It is not by accident or coincidence that Jesus chose a mountainside as the setting for His life-changing and history-making call to the twelve men who were to turn the world upside down—a memorable place for a most memorable occasion. Scripture does not tell us which mountainside Jesus chose, but, having been to Galilee many times, I can tell you that He had several awe-inspiring choices: the elevation from which He preached the Sermon on the Mount, the promontory behind the modern city of Tiberias, or even the Golan Heights with its view of the entire Sea of Galilee. Any of these would have provided a breathtaking, unforgettable setting for this pivotal moment in the lives of His followers. I imagine that many times after this, one disciple might have said to another, "Remember the mountainside? Remember when He called us? That was really something, wasn't it?" All leaders and would-be leaders should think very carefully about the setting—the *place*—for important occasions with followers.

Two occasions in my own business life underscore this for me. Before beginning my career in professional sports with the Miami Dolphins, my boss wanted me to spend time with the late Bill Veeck, who had become a legend as the owner of the Cleveland Indians and Chicago White Sox; his daring and innovative promotions provided the foundation for modern sports marketing and management.

My meeting with Mr. Veeck could have been held anywhere, in any number of very forgettable hotels.

Instead, my boss wisely arranged for me to go to the Veeck home on Maryland's eastern shore. There, in his beautiful home beside the Chesapeake Bay, surrounded by a lifetime of memorabilia from a spectacular sports career, Bill Veeck spoke to me about the challenges and opportunities I would encounter with the Dolphins. This was a high for me, in part because the setting was so memorable.

Donald Dell, who won the Davis Cup twice as the captain of the U.S. tennis team, has been my friend and business partner for many years. When he wanted to solidify our partnership, he invited my wife and me to meet him and his wife at The Greenbriar, a gracious and beautiful resort in White Sulphur Springs, West Virginia. Again, we could have met anywhere; there are many airport hotels much easier to get to than The Greenbriar, tucked into beautiful rural mountains. Though it occurred more than twenty-five years ago, I can still remember walking with Donald along the peaceful paths of The Greenbriar's grounds, stopping to sit under its stately oaks as we talked and dreamed about the partnership we would form and the business life we would share. The setting was important to the success of that occasion, providing inspirational memories that would never have been ours had we met in a more mundane setting.

When Jesus came, He invaded both time and space. As you lead, remember the great importance of both time *and* place.

CHAPTER 22

AUTHORITY, THE STUFF OF LEADERSHIP

MARK 3:14

He appointed twelve—designating them apostles—

that they might be with him and

that he might send them out to preach and

to have authority to drive out demons.

Mark 3:14–15

Leadership is largely about authority—acquiring it, using it, and investing it in others.

Leadership is *not* about issuing directives as a sort of traffic cop controlling the flow of action; that is a more managerial function. Leaders should attempt to replicate themselves, pulling followers along so that they can, more and more, act on their own to advance the cause. Visionaries anticipate the time when they will not be around, a time when followers *must* become leaders themselves if the cause is to go forward.

Jesus acquired authority from His Father, the power of His teaching, the uniqueness of His acts, and the force of who He was. He primarily used His authority as an investment in those around Him, teaching and inspiring them to act in His name, for His sake. That this was brilliant leadership is authenticated every day as millions around the world *continue* to act in His name and for His sake.

Leadership is lacking when it is not invested in followers in a way that empowers them to independently advance the cause. If a pastor is not producing congregation members who *can* and *do* "cast out demons," he has not learned, or is not appropriating, the leadership lessons of Jesus. A pastor may be a brilliant organizer and a compelling pulpiteer, but if none who attend his church are acquiring or using the authority that Jesus wants each of His followers to have, he fails the leadership test.

The wise leader brings together a group of followers who will give back to him or her. Mark says that Jesus appointed the twelve "that they might be with him." The cliché about being lonely at the top represents a leadership failure; the very best leaders are not lonely because they have developed an intimacy with a close group of followers. Are you producing a group of followers who are "with" you, who help to sustain you as you lead them?

Just as Jesus used special times and places to impact His leadership, He also used symbols in a powerful and compelling way. It is no coincidence that He appointed twelve apostles rather than ten or fourteen. The twelve represent the twelve tribes of Israel; the number has meaning and a message. Symbols are powerful. Give great thought to logos, titles, mottoes, and mission statements. They have significant and lasting impact. Use them as a part of your leadership strategy.

CHAPTER 23

PAINFUL ATTACKS ON YOUR LEADERSHIP
MARK 3:20–21

When his family heard about this,

they went to take charge of him,

for they said, "He is out of his mind."

Mark 3:21

The above passage is one of the most poignant in all of Scripture in the discussion of leadership because it delineates the significant price leaders often pay.

Withstanding an expected attack from enemies is one thing; even dissension among the ranks of followers, while no fun, is an anticipated part of leadership. But when our families don't believe in us, that hurts—

deeply. Consider how Jesus must have felt on this occasion. He had pulled together a group of followers, performed miracles of healing, and attracted large crowds; yet His own family said, "We have to take charge of Him. He is out of His mind." That's a tough one.

Yet leadership at the highest level almost always demands such a compelling vision that even those closest to us may question our wisdom, even our sanity. This questioning may even serve as a checkpoint for a potential decision: if no one whom I respect will question this decision, how can I be sure it is right?

Contemplate this situation. If you aspire to leadership, see if you can pass this test: "If my family says I'm nuts, can I still go on?" Obviously Jesus did, but certainly not without pain.

It is important to realize that there is nothing disgraceful or shameful about failing this or any other tests of leadership; not everyone is called to be a leader. After all, for leaders to succeed, there must be followers. Most of us need to be good, dedicated followers in our earthly pursuits. *All* of us need to be good, dedicated followers of the Lord Jesus. In God's sight, leaders are not more highly valued than followers. He loves us all.

In my own business career, I think I was often at my best as a follower. I became the president of my company and was thrust into leadership responsibilities; but as I look back on forty years in business, I feel I was at my very best as a follower, doing my most productive work as a number-two man, serving a leader I admired and respected.

There is no tragedy in failing to become a leader *if* we face up to the possibility of leadership squarely, honestly, and in an attitude of submission to God's will. If we prayerfully examine opportunities to lead and are then obedient, we will be successful as either a leader or a follower. Tragedies occur when we fail to take on leadership responsibilities that we are clearly called to fulfill, or when we pursue or demand leadership responsibilities without objectively and prayerfully examining our ability to lead. When either of these occur, people are hurt, resources are wasted, and good opportunities for growth are retarded.

Are you willing to pay the high price of leadership? Examine yourself—see if you really can or want to be a leader. Ask God to guide you.

CHAPTER 24

LEADERS
TELL STORIES

So Jesus called them

and spoke to them in parables.

Mark 3:23

The most effective communicators have been great storytellers, from Aesop to Jesus to Abraham Lincoln to Mark Twain to Garrison Keillor to Ronald Reagan. Why? Everyone loves a story. Stories are like windows to the truth.

In his landmark book on corporate leadership, *In Search of Excellence*, Tom Peters illustrates the effectiveness of leading by telling stories. Leading through storytelling requires more than just spinning yarns; the stories must make important, relevant points. Through parables Jesus imparted many of His most vital messages. Leaders need to appreciate this impact and prepare their own repertoire of parables that relate to their own particular enterprises.

Wayne Callaway became a very effective chairman of PepsiCo. I got to know him when we were both living in Dallas and he was running Frito-Lay, one of PepsiCo's biggest and most successful divisions. Most of corporate America attributes Frito-Lay's success to its legendary distribution system, legendary because—according to Wayne—the leadership of Frito-Lay very carefully, very deliberately told and retold stories of their distribution people going to extraordinary lengths to ensure that Frito-Lay products reached customers despite any difficult circumstances. These stories, told and retold, made heroes of those distribution people, made other Frito-Lay employees want to emulate them, and, most importantly, established a corporate culture that celebrated quality service.

Jesus both established and perfected the use of parables as a leadership methodology. Just think of the heroes He created who continue to inspire us—the good Samaritan, the good and faithful servant, the wise virgins, the poor widow, and others. As a leader, you need to teach through relevant stories that create heroes, build legends, and help establish the kind of culture that inspires your followers to excellence.

Build up others through the stories you tell. Jesus was not the hero of the parables He told; others were. Too many tell stories of which they are the hero. Make others the heroes of your stories, not yourself. If you aim to be a hero, do what it takes to be the hero of stories others tell.

Jesus taught in many ways, but the wonderful stories He used are great examples of conveying important lessons in memorable ways. Wise leaders will take note.

CHAPTER 25

UNITY, A LEADERSHIP REQUIREMENT

MARK 3:23–27

"If a house is divided against itself,

that house cannot stand."

Mark 3:25

Quality leadership produces unity, and wise leadership is willing to sacrifice in order to build unity.

I had the privilege of being a college athlete. During four years of eligibility, I played on two quite different kinds of college basketball teams, different not so much in talent but in degrees of unity. Playing a long season on a team racked by dissension among players was not much fun and caused much of the joy of playing to be lost. The unified teams on which I played produced some of my most treasured memories and most enduring relationships.

Successful coaches often get rid of very talented players who cause disunity. The remaining players, though less talented, are often more successful. Unity means so much. There is no substitute for it. It is a prerequisite to sustained success.

Unity rarely just happens. It has to be sought and taught. In my basketball experience, the leadership that produced most of the team's unity came from a player rather than from the coach; the titular leader is not always the one who instills unity in his or her team. Conversely, unity can be easily destroyed by almost anyone. A wise leader does all he or she can to build with those who contribute to unity while eliminating the causes of disunity from the team.

When Jesus said that a house divided against itself cannot stand, He spoke a truth applicable to every kind of human endeavor. Unity is essential. Don't be afraid to eliminate the source of disunity from your enterprise—it's your responsibility as a leader.

CHAPTER 26

LEADERS ARE OFTEN UNAPPRECIATED

MARK 3:30

He said this because they were saying,

"He has an evil spirit."

Mark 3:30

Jesus showed us that even when we work exclusively for the welfare of others, some may say we are evil. In the instance Mark describes, the Pharisees deliberately twisted the words and deeds of Jesus to make them appear evil.

The same thing happens to leaders today, even to those with the best motives and the highest standards. You will never be fairly judged at all times. It is possible to do nothing but good and *still* be attacked. Don't expect fairness in a fallen world.

Winston Churchill was perhaps the greatest leader of the twentieth century. His magnificent, courageous leadership of the British people during the darkest days of World War 2 inspired freedom-loving people everywhere. Yet, in the first election after his leadership helped to secure victory over the Nazis, he was immediately voted out of office! This is an example of what leaders often face. Universal appreciation doesn't always follow great leadership.

CHAPTER 27

SPECIAL
RELATIONSHIPS
————— MARK 3:31–35 —————

"Whoever does God's will is

my brother and sister and mother."

Mark 3:35

Leaders have special relationships with their followers and special responsibilities to them. When a leader beckons someone to follow, he or she asks to be responsible for an aspect of that person's life.

The life of Jesus and His involvement with followers demonstrates the intensity to which the leader/follower relationship can grow; it doesn't replace family relationships, but it can become just as strong. Obviously, the nature of the enterprise will dictate the intensity of the relationship. Coaching a youth soccer team is considerably different from leading troops into battle during wartime.

Jesus, the greatest of all leaders, clearly represents the special relationship that can evolve between leaders and followers. He never exhibited a cool detachment toward His followers; they were not simply pawns to carry out His wishes and implement His plans. His followers were very special to Him and, conversely, He was very special to them. This mutually caring, mutually productive, mutually protective, nonexploitive leader/follower relationship that Jesus maintained with His disciples is a model for all leaders and followers.

The idea that leaders should treat all followers exactly the same is a myth; trying to do this actually inhibits the kind of intimacy necessary for the most positive type of leadership to emerge. In order to lead a large number effectively, it is always necessary to have a deeper, more personal, more intense relationship with a small inner circle of followers.

In this passage we find that Jesus specifically called those "seated in a circle around him" His mother and His brothers. Although there is no doubt that He had a very special relationship with the twelve He called to be apostles and—of these twelve, an even closer relationship with Peter, James, and John—He really includes *all* of His followers in this intimate promise of a special relationship.

Good leaders have a vision; better leaders share a vision; the best leaders invite others to join them in spreading this vision. In this way, the best leaders create a sense of intimacy with hundreds, thousands, and even millions of followers, which explains why some feel that they know great world leaders even though they have never met. Shared vision binds leaders and followers together in a way that little else can.

CHAPTER 28

YOU WIN SOME; YOU LOSE SOME

MARK 4:1-9

"Still other seed fell on good soil."

Mark 4:8

According to an old baseball cliché, "You win some. You lose some. And some get rained out." A wise leader will understand the implications of this for his or her leadership.

Every leader would like to win them all, but this is impossible; no one wins more than "some." It is also important to understand the "rainouts," those people and circumstances for which there will be another day; they are neither won nor lost, but will be in the future. They need to be remembered and "rescheduled" for the most opportune time and should not be written off or forgotten. A time will come for them. A good leader understands this and plans accordingly.

Because the sower couldn't know in advance where to find the best soil, he had to sow (e.g., "broadcast") the seed in all directions in order to guarantee that some would land on good soil. After all the marketing plans are made and the strategy is set, no one knows what will happen in the marketplace. All things being equal, however, the more you produce, the more you advertise, and the more you sell. The sower was willing to take a 75 percent "loss" in order to reap a 25 percent "profit," which actually yielded a hundredfold dividend.

Leaders who can't handle rejection, defeat, or delay don't last. Leaders who have to win everything *every time* are short-lived with limited success. Leaders must believe that if they sow good seed, *some* will fall on good soil. *Some* will produce good things. Even though they may not see good results immediately or even in their lifetime, Jesus teaches us that good seed *will* produce good fruit. We can't be discouraged by a lack of response, but we must trust God to bring about the harvest in His own time and His own way.

CHAPTER 29

TRUTH
AND TIMING
MARK 4:1–20

When he was alone,

the Twelve and the others around him

asked him about the parables.

Mark 4:10

To be effective over the long haul, a leader must speak the truth at all times. However, he or she may need to reserve some of the truth for those in an inner circle.

A leader's inner circle is defined by how much of the truth is shared with each prospective member. In the case of Jesus, He spoke to the multitudes and taught His disciples, but He reserved the most compelling truth for Peter, James, and John.

The truth shared with each group is very important in the way it is shared, in its content, and in its timing. The wonderful parables Jesus shared with the multitudes were undoubtedly carefully prepared, finely honed, and presented with precision and power, no less important than the message shared with His disciples, just different in degree. It's ironic that Jesus spoke in parables as much to conceal the truth as to reveal it, illustrated by verse 12: "They may indeed see but not perceive" (RSV). The parables are like a thermometer of the soul, revealing something of a person's spiritual perception (or lack thereof). That's why Jesus kept saying, "He who has ears to hear, let him hear." Not everyone has "ears" attuned to the truth of God, but some do. These quaint stories reveal as much about the hearer as they do the speaker.

When we set out to build the worldwide professional tennis tour, there were many competing interests. We had to carefully craft a message for the media to disseminate around the world; we had to articulate a more detailed message to the players of the world; and there was a very small, intimate group with which all of the plans and dreams for the future of tennis were shared. All of the messages were true and consistent, but each group received a different part of the truth at a different time. At the appropriate time all the interested parties were given all the available information and everyone knew all there was to know. The same is true of Jesus' message. He shared it differently, at different times during His time on earth, but now we all have equal access to it through Scripture.

A leader errs when he or she tells too much too soon to those not ready for it. A leader also errs by failing to assemble a small group who knows the very heartbeat of the vision and message. A wise leader will think carefully and pray earnestly about what, when, and how to release information.

CHAPTER 30

LEADERSHIP EXPECTATIONS

MARK 4:10–25

"Others, like seed sown on good soil,

hear the word, accept it, and produce a crop—

thirty, sixty or even a hundred times what was sown."

Mark 4:20

The wonderful parable of the sower is a lesson about expectations. A wise leader will have realistic expectations about the receipt of his message and will keep the expectations of his followers firmly in check.

Jesus knew that even the very best message—eternal life as a gift of grace—would be rejected by most people, and He began very early to prepare His disciples for this. Unrealistic expectations produce disillusionment—a killer of any enterprise.

It's always important to emphasize the "up side" in communicating with followers. While keeping expectations real and preparing for the tough times is important, it is vital to show followers the potential fruit of staying the course, of being faithful to the mission. Both leaders and followers must believe in the thirty-sixty-one hundred multiple to persevere and hold steady.

We saw the parable of the sower played out in the construction of the Superdome in New Orleans. Without wise leadership this great stadium, which has proven to be such a boon to the city, would never have been built. At first, many saw the significant benefits of the stadium, but as the costs and difficulties were considered, many believers fell away. Some turned against the project as jealousies and greed were given free reign in their lives.

The two men most responsible for this huge project—Dave Dixon, who created the idea, and then-governor John McKiethen—could easily have become disillusioned and abandoned the project. As an assistant to Dave and the governor, I could easily have been discouraged as some of the state's major newspapers vehemently turned on the project, but Dave kept me and everyone else on a steady course.

The opposition, many of whom attacked him personally, did not discourage him, and he did not allow it to discourage me. Dave realistically expected opposition yet continued to articulate the benefits of success—the thirty-sixty-one hundred multiple. This is leadership. The result of this kind of leadership is a great stadium, one that will continue to benefit the state of Louisiana for decades to come.

Sow your seed. Have realistic expectations. Don't let discouragers discourage you—and enjoy the harvest.

CHAPTER 31

PUBLICITY, PUBLIC RELATIONS, AND LEADERSHIP

MARK 4:21–23

"Do you bring in a lamp

to put it under a bowl or a bed?"

Mark 4:21

The Gospels have much to say about publicity and public relations.

The phenomenon of John the Baptist points us to the legitimacy of these activities when they are pursued in the best way, for the best ends. In opposition to the sincere, truthful efforts of John the Baptist (which were not self-serving or self-aggrandizing, but for the good of the mission) are those of the hypocritical Pharisees, who sought to portray a false image of what they did and who they were in order to gain unde-served praise.

Jesus wants the world to know who we are, who we *truly* are. A leader will understand this and make every effort to ensure that this happens by first ensuring that his followers know who he is and what he is about. Jesus did this by often questioning His disciples about Himself and His mission to be sure that their under-standing constantly increased.

He also wanted the world to know the truth of His identity and His mission, employing the publicity methods of His day to accomplish this, starting with John the Baptist. If He had not hoped to disseminate His mission or message, He would have stayed in one place to teach His disciples. Instead, He traveled con-stantly, teaching and preaching in all sorts of venues to all sorts of people.

Several years ago, the Mercedes Benz automobile company ran ads describing a brand-new technology to help cars absorb the impact of a front-end collision. Although they owned the rights to the revolutionary technology, they freely shared it with other car compa-nies in the interest of promoting safety. The tag line of the ad consisted of these thought-provoking words: *Some things in life are too important not to share.* In the same way, a leader must ensure that his "good news" isn't the "world's best kept secret." A wise leader will see the mission at the center of his efforts.

CHAPTER 32

EVALUATE

"Consider carefully what you hear,"

he continued. "With the measure you use,

it will be measured to you—and even more."

Mark 4:24

Effective leaders constantly evaluate their followers.

They must look for substance and avoid being fooled by the person who spends more time trying to look good than doing good. The larger the organization, the more difficult this becomes and the more important it is for leaders to discern the difference between solid performance and fluff. It is important to evaluate effort in order to give those who *do* perform added responsibility, thereby increasing their value to both the enterprise and to themselves.

Few things are more damaging to morale and to bottom-line results than failure of leadership to properly evaluate employees. When a person does an outstanding job without ever receiving bigger, more important, more rewarding responsibilities, it is discouraging. Perhaps even more discouraging is when leadership is gulled into giving credit to an undeserving person rather than the real performer.

Jesus tells us that he who is given responsibility and knowledge should use it productively, after which he should be given more. If a person does not use what he has, even this should be taken from him. To make this work—and it will work fairly for all—consistent, thorough, ongoing evaluation is necessary to ensure that each team member, as well as the enterprise itself, reaches its full potential.

Jesus repeatedly teaches that it is not how much we have that counts, but what we do with what we have. Leaders must help followers understand this principle and hold them accountable to it.

CHAPTER 33

A LEADER
IS FAITHFUL
———— MARK 4:26–29 ————

"Night and day, whether he sleeps or gets up,

the seed sprouts and grows,

though he does not know how."

Mark 4:27

God is faithful. He expects all of us, particularly His leaders, to be faithful as well.

Just as there is order and consistency in the world God has created for us, there should be order and consistency in our leadership. We need to be faithful to our followers by articulating a clear, consistent message that states understandable goals and faithfully rewards those who help us reach our goals.

Nothing erodes a leader's effectiveness more than unfaithfulness. I know of a company whose leader constantly changes the playing field, earning him a reputation for unfaithfulness. He rigs the company's fiscal year results and employees' evaluation criteria to work in favor of the company's short-term bottom line, hurting everyone in the long run by his unfaithfulness. Employee turnover is high, and the company has been stagnant for several years. God's rules apply not only to the seasons—to planting and harvesting—but also to human relationships, business, and leadership.

Jesus teaches us that we cannot "beat the system." We may not understand how God's plan works, but we can know that He is faithful. We can know that if we lead faithfully He will bless our leadership efforts. We may not always "win" as the world measures winning, but as we plant good seed, a good harvest will result. Leaders are called to faithfulness more than they are called to success.

LITTLE THINGS— IMPORTANT THINGS

MARK 4:30–32

"It is like a mustard seed,

which is the smallest seed

you plant in the ground."

Mark 4:31

"Little Things Mean a Lot," the old Teresa Brewer song, might well be a theme song for leaders. More importantly, Jesus' parable of the mustard seed could easily be called a parable for leaders.

Leaders must understand that little things *do* mean a lot and that everything they do is magnified in the minds of those they lead; every word, gesture, smile, or frown takes on added significance when it comes from a leader. A follower's day can be ruined without a word of greeting from his or her leader. Conversely, a follower can be inspired and energized by the slightest positive comment from a leader.

When Tom Peters writes about "management by walking around," his writing is based on this understanding. Leaders need to be aware of the effect they have on those they lead. Successful leaders, from great football coaches to great generals, understand this and make their "little" contacts really count.

General Eisenhower spent the last few hours before D-Day mingling, not with the top brass, but with the soldiers, sailors, and airmen who were about to invade Europe. He knew that even though he could only visit a few outfits, word of his visits would spread like wildfire among the enlisted men, giving them courage to face the onslaught of Nazi defenders. Don't become so preoccupied with thoughts of leadership that you fail to plant the "mustard seed" that will grow into a great, worthwhile relationship between you and those you lead. Be sensitive. Be alert.

In the parable of the mustard seed, Jesus also teaches leaders that big things can grow from small beginnings. One has only to consider ideas such as

Scotch Tape and Post-It Notes, which grew into multi-million-dollar products for 3M because leaders recognized the potential in small beginnings. Great ideas and great people have emerged from small beginnings. Seemingly unimpressive people can impact the world with the spark of a brilliant idea.

The Bible often celebrates small things. It was little David, not the giant Goliath. It was Gideon's small band, not the enemy hordes. It was the widow's mite, not the Pharisee's largesse. It was the cup of cold water in His name, not the grandstand play. Sometimes it's better to "think small."

Most importantly, the mustard seed parable is about faith. The most important faith any of us can have is in our Lord, who promises that even the tiniest faith can cause great things to happen. Faith is an important component of successful leadership. By definition, followers must have faith in their leader; if they don't, they are not true followers and there is no true leader. When a follower puts faith in his or her leader, the leader should see this as a sacred trust. However, even the wisest leader will not always make the best decision or chart the best plans.

In making a poor decision or in executing a bad plan, a leader will not destroy a follower's faith *if* it is apparent that the motives were good and that the leader was trying hard to do the right thing for the enterprise. Followers do not demand perfection, but they do expect and should receive honesty. An honest leader keeps followers' faith intact.

A wise leader will build faith in those he leads by giving individuals greater and greater responsibility and latitude as they demonstrate greater and greater capability and understanding. The mustard seed principle works in this regard. A little faith shown by a leader in a follower can grow into a great, productive relationship.

CHAPTER 35

LEADERSHIP CALMS THE STORM

He said to his disciples,

"Why are you so afraid?

Do you still have no faith?"

Mark 4:40

A leader *must* be the calm in the storm.

Turbulent times are sure to come, and when they do it is imperative for a leader to be a calming, steadying influence. Many appear impressive when everyone is cheering, but a storm is always the true test of leadership mettle. Be ready for the storm; be ready to calm those around you in its midst.

Being the calm at the center of a storm does not mean being detached or unrealistic. It does mean moving deliberately and positively to handle the situation, instilling faith, and driving out unwarranted fear. Restate your mission to let your followers know what you are trying to do is both worthwhile and doable. Reciting past successes often helps: "Remember when the wolf was at our door before and how we got through it?" is the kind of recitation that can rally the troops.

Visible, palpable panic is the telltale sign that the wrong person was given a leadership role. Working with the live telecasts of major sports events is tantamount to living in the eye of the storm. Many things can go wrong to knock the telecast off the air or cause it to go on at less than its best. The director is the leader and, in a big telecast, has hundreds of followers at his command, connected to each of his men and women by an audio line. If cameras go out, the satellite goes dark, a main power line is severed, or something goes wrong at the network, the director must control the situation by what he says and *how* he says it. When things start going wrong in a live telecast with millions watching around the world and millions of dollars at stake, a calm leader is a great asset.

I sat in one of our big production trucks at the U.S. Open when things started to go bad, and I saw the director, literally drenched in sweat, keep a voice as calm and reassuring as if he was at his grandmother's house: "Guys, camera three has stopped functioning. We will cover with the overhead until it is back up. Give me some good close-ups with that one," or "The Network is not receiving our feed. We will keep the tape rolling and give them the highlights when they are back up and running." No problem. Another day at the office. Everyone remains calm and the job gets done.

Unfortunately, I have also seen the opposite happen. At a big event at Madison Square Garden in New York, I saw our director panic, rip his headphones off, and instigate a shoving match with one of the crew. As far as I know, he never directed another live telecast.

Even the most experienced leaders may sometimes falter under pressure; many of the disciples were seasoned fishermen who had been in this very situation many times before, yet they panicked.

Just as Jesus calmed both the physical storm and the storms in the hearts of His followers, leadership today requires the same kind of effort. We can never control nature in the way Jesus did, and we can never speak words of assurance with the kind of authority He commanded. However, we need to emulate His methods to the extent we can so that we are ready when the storm hits, even the unexpected one.

We need to control our own fears and repress any impulse to panic. We need to speak words of reassurance in a calming tone, addressing the problem in a deliberate, measured, effective way. We need to *lead* through adverse circumstances, not be overcome by them.

Nothing will raise a leader in the eyes of his or her followers more than when he or she effectively handles a crisis. Calm, effective leadership in the midst of a storm will do more to establish a leader than most any situation. A wise, well-prepared leader may even hope for a crisis in order to prove his leadership skills.

It was certainly no accident that Jesus was in a boat with His disciples when a storm arose. We certainly don't advocate creating a crisis for the sake of solving it, but we do feel you should be thankful for one when it comes. As James 1:2 says, "Count it all joy." In the same way that the awestruck disciples wondered about Jesus' identity after He miraculously calmed the winds and the waves, your followers will speak of you with greater respect after you have led them through a storm.

CHAPTER 36

FLEXIBILITY

Then the people began

to plead with Jesus

to leave their region.

Mark 5:17

Leadership is a complex undertaking, involving both steadfast determination and thoughtful flexibility. An unwillingness to change (particularly a schedule) has caused a myriad of leadership failures. Quality leadership almost always requires strategic retreats.

Our company is involved in the production and worldwide distribution of television programming, beginning more than twenty-five years ago with tennis events. With its relatively long history of involvement with both England and the United States, Japan was a natural market for tennis programming. In the 1970s Korea was also emerging as an economic power in the region. My partner and I determined we would take our tennis programming there as well.

The Koreans had almost no interest in tennis, however, and no amount of effort could persuade their television executives that tennis would succeed in their market. In this instance, unlike some others, we were smart enough to beat a strategic retreat, returning to that market several years later and putting tennis on Korean television with great success. We were smart enough to adjust to *their* schedule, not try to force ours on them. When the Gadarenes pled with Jesus to leave their region, He didn't argue with them—He left.

Jesus showed us that it is sometimes necessary to "cut our losses," to change our schedule, or alter our plans. In Gadara He could have said, "Are you as demented as the wild man was before I came? I just worked a great miracle benefiting one of your own and, ultimately, your whole society. Don't you want to know more, to experience more of this kind of power?" He didn't. He left. He saw that this "market" was not ready and He left; He "cut His losses" and went into areas more central and more strategically important to His core mission.

Jesus exercised great leadership in refusing to be bogged down where returns would be small. Pride and ego didn't keep Him there. He didn't say, "I'll show them." Leaving a market, product, partnership, or business alliance can often be a critical strategic move. When we fail to make these moves decisively, it is usually because pride and ego impair our judgment. You don't have to let this happen to you.

CHAPTER 37

PUBLICITY

So the man went away and began to tell

in the Decapolis how much Jesus had done

for him. And all the people were amazed.

Mark 5:20

Very early in my professional sports administration career I learned the difference between advertising and publicity, as well as their relative worth.

In the most basic sense, advertising is what you say about yourself, and publicity is what others say about you. Advertising is always discounted in the minds of those to whom it is directed. People intuitively know that advertising is self-serving and paints the best possible picture of those who buy the advertising, typically taking it with the proverbial grain of salt.

On the other hand, publicity, depending—to a degree—on the reputation and credibility of the disseminating organ, can have more of an impact. A favorable story in the *New York Times* by a respected columnist obviously has a greater effect than one in the *National Enquirer* by a writer of questionable integrity. Publicity—because of its greater credibility—is inherently more valuable than advertising.

The most potent kind of publicity is the first-person account. The person who can say, "This happened to me. I was there," is a very powerful publicity agent. Jesus put this publicity principle into practice when, after casting the demons out of the man, He did not let the man accompany Him but instructed him to go and tell his family how much the Lord had done for him. The man not only told his family, but also went into the ten cities of the region telling about Jesus and the mighty work He had done, thus becoming one of the all-time great publicity agents.

By leaving the man behind, Jesus accomplished more than if He had stayed there Himself, enabling a "retreat" to become an "advance" for the kingdom of God. As a living "before and after" example of the power of Jesus, the man was much more valuable in his home area than he would have been traveling with Jesus and the disciples. People who had seen him as a wild, naked demoniac could now see him clothed and in his right mind—and the man gave all the credit to Jesus. Powerful testimony. Powerful publicity. Powerful leadership.

It is vital that leaders understand the importance of strategically placing their team members. Jesus knew that the demon-free advocate would be a more powerful force for good in his home area than in places where he was unknown. Some leaders keep all their key people with them at all times, a practice that hinders the spread of the Word and the growth of the enterprise. Do like Jesus did—place them strategically.

CHAPTER 38

DECISIVE ACTION

So Jesus went with him.

Mark 5:24

A quality leader acts decisively when the occasion calls for it—decisively, not impulsively.

In this situation, Jesus had all the facts necessary to act intelligently and helpfully. He didn't need to call a committee meeting or take a vote among His disciples—"All those in favor of going to help Jairus's daughter, raise your right hand." None of that. Neither did He tell Jairus, "I'll get back to you on that;" nor did He say, "Get me more information." He responded. He went. He moved. He acted. He led.

Jairus was credible. He was a leader of the synagogue, someone Jesus probably knew. He certainly made the right approach, one of great respect and faith. "So Jesus went with him." Great leadership is responsive leadership acting on quality information.

Great leadership is also courageous. When the news reached Him that Jairus's daughter had worsened and died, it would have been easy for Him to say, "I am so sorry. You reached me too late. I wish I could have helped." He didn't do this. When everything seemed lost, He continued to respond, act, and help. This is courageous and prudent leadership. Jesus *knew* what the situation was and *knew* He had the power to correct it.

No leader can do it all; in fact, no leader can do most of it. But good leaders understand the value of symbolic action. Jesus practiced this principle by "picking His spots" to maximize the educational benefit to His disciples. By accompanying Jairus, He showed His disciples that even the Son of God—*especially* the Son of God—has time for people who hurt, a lesson they would remember years later.

Obviously, none of us will ever have the wisdom, insight, or power of Jesus. However, He can be a model of leadership—in this instance, of responsive, cogent, decisive, courageous leadership—acting on quality information and continuing to move forward in the face of what appeared to be disaster.

CHAPTER 39

LEADERSHIP IS EXPENSIVE

"Who touched my clothes?"

Mark 5:30

Leadership is expensive. As a leader, there is always a price to pay.

Just as Jesus realized "that power had gone out from him" when the woman touched Him in search of a miracle, potential leaders need to understand that leadership is a draining experience. Even as Jesus performed this wonderful act of healing, He felt the cost. The context in which this event occurs helps illuminate the cost of leadership.

As the woman touched Him, Jesus was already on His way to deal with an urgent situation. As soon as

He arrived He was swarmed by crowds and, after stepping ashore, was met with a critical situation that demanded His attention—only *some* of the costs of Jesus' leadership. The demands on your time and attention are very high, often leaving little time for yourself. But Mark's mention of the fact that Jesus felt power leave Him at the woman's touch is most telling; a leader does not, *cannot*, help others without giving of himself or herself. Leadership is costly.

————— CHAPTER 40 —————

PREPARING
SUCCESSORS

————— MARK 5:35–43 —————

He did not let anyone follow

him except Peter, James

and John the brother of James.

Mark 5:37

Wise leaders plan, from the very inception of their leadership, for the time when they will no longer be around.

It is almost a business school cliché that a leader's first task is to ensure that the best possible replacement is being trained and prepared to step in when he or she can no longer lead. While the admonition is so logical and so frequently repeated, I am struck by how seldom it is practiced. Jesus, the wisest leader of all, certainly didn't make that mistake, telling His disciples almost from the moment He called them that He would not always be with them. He wisely began to focus quite narrowly on those few who would be most capable of leadership when He was no longer there.

Unfortunately, even with the perfect example Jesus set for us and with all the leadership lessons others try to teach us, there are still far too many examples of huge vacuums being left as a leader departs.

Sadly, this happens often with churches. I know of one great south Florida church that has never been the same since the departure of its dynamic senior pastor several years ago; no plan for succession was in place, leaving a vacuum that remains to this day. You only have to read a current issue of the *Wall Street Journal* to find accounts of the same thing happening to businesses. Corporate leaders act as if they will always be there, and when the inevitable happens, no one is prepared to step in, thereby creating disarray, dismay, and disappointment.

Christian leaders have a particular responsibility to plan for succession and the future of their enterprise. If they are to be good stewards of the leadership responsibility God has given them, they must do their best to prepare their own well-trained, experienced Peter, James, and John to smoothly and seamlessly assume command when they move on.

Thankfully, we also have some positive examples. Although this succession is still being played out, it seems that careful, prayerful planning has paved the way for Franklin Graham to gracefully assume the ministry responsibilities of his father, Billy Graham. It is fitting that Billy Graham will cap off his wonderfully productive life of service by following so closely the example of the One he has consistently followed.

Jesus trained and prepared the most successful leadership team of all time. Their achievements after Jesus' departure prove that leadership can be passed on by adequately investing in a plan for succession. Be a good leader. Be a good steward of your leadership by preparing for the inevitable time when you will no longer lead.

CHAPTER 41

PRACTICAL VISION

He gave strict orders not to let anyone

know about this and told them

to give her something to eat.

Mark 5:43

"Visionary leader" can either serve as a complimentary description or relegate someone into the "dreamer" category—a person who sees the big picture but misses the smaller, important things.

Certainly a leader needs to understand and commit to a strategic plan, but big plans and brilliant strategy are always held captive to tactics and execution; if your alarm clock doesn't go off and you can't get your car to start, your big presentation on the future direction of the company might not happen. The ideal leader combines vision with the kind of common sense that makes his vision a reality.

Obviously, Jesus was this kind of leader. When He said, "Give her something to eat," He demonstrated leadership through the completion of His thoughts. A lesser leader, after performing such a miraculous healing, might have done any number of things—made a speech, posed for pictures, or accepted the plaudits of witnesses—but Jesus said, "Give her something to eat." Fortunately, Peter, James, and John were present to absorb the lesson, one they surely never forgot. After Pentecost, Peter—by then the group's leader—was careful to meet the more practical needs of the early church, while prayer, worship, and teaching moved the group forward spiritually. The best leaders are visionary *and* practical.

In this fallen world, the wisest, most successful leaders analyze their strengths and weaknesses and act accordingly. If you are a big thinker with the ability to visualize, make sure you surround yourself with people blessed with practical talent. If your leadership style is more practical, be sure to assemble a "brain trust" to complete some of the long-range planning and dreaming. It is not necessary for you to have it all, only to have access to it all.

The key is quality, prayerful, clear-eyed self-analysis. Don't convince yourself that you are strongly practical when you are not. If you fail to say the equivalent of "give her something to eat" when the situation demands it, make sure you have someone by your side who will whisper in your ear. If your style is to focus quite narrowly on the task at hand, be sure to have access to someone who thinks about tomorrow. This is the way staffs should be built—to complement the strengths of the leader and cover his or her weaknesses.

Consider the way a head coach in the National Football League builds his staff. If he loves defense and has a proclivity for defensive strategy, he doesn't surround himself with more defensive coaching talent. Rather, his top assistant is likely to be an offensive specialist. On some staffs, if the head coach is more of a theoretical strategist, his top assistant might be an organizer, a detail-oriented person.

Don't be discouraged by Jesus' perfection. Work hard to emulate it. Don't be afraid to get help with those areas outside your natural strengths while working to improve areas of weakness.

CHAPTER 42

THE BEST
AND THE WORST

MARK 6:1–5

And they took offense at him.

Mark 6:3

Leadership brings out both the best and the worst in people. Wise leaders understand this, accepting it as a natural part of leadership, and try to emphasize the best and minimize the worst.

Recognize that your motives will always be questioned by some and that, even when you are performing at your very best, creating the most good for the most people, some will "take offense." Unfortunately, those offended will often be people closest to you or those you have known the longest. Just as the people of Nazareth refused to see Jesus as anything other than a carpenter, in spite of the wisdom of His teaching and His miracles of healing, some will never recognize any leadership talent. Here is a classic example: One of Mark Twain's boyhood friends, jealous of the writer's fame, said, "I know just as many stories as Mark Twain. All he did was write them down."

When I was a young college baseball coach, my team played exceptionally, and I was named "Coach of the Year" in my state. One of my oldest friends celebrated my good fortune with me, while another remarked, "Being the baseball Coach of the Year in Michigan is no big deal. Michigan is not a great college baseball state." Some celebrate with you; some don't. This is a reality of leadership.

Recognize that you will probably be at your most productive away from "home." The old saying "take that show on the road" is one to consider; staying close to home has its comforts and rewards, but it also has its limitations and constrictions.

Jesus did less in Nazareth than anywhere else because of the hometown attitude toward Him. He limited Himself, and the Scripture says, "He could not do any miracles there, except lay his hands on a few sick people and heal them"—amazing in and of itself, but that is miniscule compared to what He could have done.

I have seen a lot of leadership talent wasted due to a refusal to leave home. Although it is good to have a strong appreciation and affection for home, returning periodically to visit as Jesus did, maximized leadership usually occurs away from home. Those who insist on staying at home often fail to fulfill their leadership potential.

Peter, James, and John did not become leaders by lingering in Capernaum on the Sea of Galilee, but by traveling to Jerusalem. "Come follow me" almost always means following away from home for maximum leadership effect, although there is nothing wrong with returning home if that is where the Lord has called you to be. For most of us, however, leaving home is a part of God's plan for our leadership.

CHAPTER 43

THE USE OF AUTHORITY

Calling the Twelve to him,

he sent them out two by two and

gave them authority over evil spirits.

Mark 6:7

Authority is *the* leadership commodity. How a leader uses his or her authority will help determine the effectiveness of that leadership.

Maximizing your authority is an elusive skill. Some try to exercise authority they have not earned and do not have, while others, paralyzed by fear or self-doubt, refuse to exercise the authority they clearly possess.

Some leaders hold their authority too closely, strangling on the demands of the mundane and the minutiae of daily life. Some delegate too broadly, dissipating the potential effects of their authority.

Jesus appropriately exercised the authority He had. His was clearly not a democratic organization. When He told His disciples to prepare a boat to cross the Sea of Galilee, He didn't first call for a committee meeting. When He decided to head for Jerusalem, He didn't call for a show of hands to see how many agreed. He exercised His authority, yet He also recognized the authority of His Father: "Yet not what I will, but what you will."

In whatever the enterprise—a home, Sunday school class, church, or business—work hard as you lead to understand the extent of your authority, and then exercise it. Be the person to stop an appropriate part of "the buck." A leader, by definition, is a "buck stopper," one who makes decisions and accepts the responsibility for them.

A wise leader will naturally want to increase his or her authority if he or she realizes how precious it is. Authority can only grow if it is first given away, strategically delegated to competent followers. If delegated unwisely, it will be wasted on those unprepared for the responsibilities that accompany it.

Jesus delegated strategically. His disciples were given the theory *and* the practice. He was careful to send them out with a limited mandate. He gave them authority to cast out evil spirits, but He did not say at that time, "Go out and save the world." For the moment their authority was limited. Later it would embrace the entire world (see Mark 16:15). They knew what authority they had, as well as the constraints they faced in exercising it. Because of Jesus' wise leadership, authority grew, and good things happened.

CHAPTER 44

LEADERSHIP
TEAMS

MARK 6:7

Calling the Twelve to him,

he sent them out two by two and

gave them authority over evil spirits.

Mark 6:7

Earlier in this book I mentioned my partner, Donald
Dell. In the early days of our relationship, we learned
that we were usually stronger and more effective as a
team than as individuals. With this in mind, we were
careful to handle the most important presentations and
the toughest negotiations together whenever possible.
When things of utmost importance are on the line, the
two of us like to tackle them together.

We learned that two was the right number for us. At times, however, we decided to take along a third or even a fourth colleague—almost always a mistake. Donald and I worked so well together that two plus one was, for us, less than two. We developed a sort of natural rhythm together; in the give and take of intense negotiations, we almost never "stepped on the other's line," enabling us to enjoy many successes.

Obviously there were times when circumstance kept us from working together. I was the first American sports executive allowed into the People's Republic of China after the end of the terrible "Cultural Revolution," but a condition of my entrance was that I must go alone—no entourage, not even my partner, could accompany me. Though it was more than twenty years ago, I still remember how off-balance I was throughout the entire visit. I was not as effective alone.

As soon as possible, I worked out another visit to China—with my partner; we were able to negotiate some breakthrough business deals, among them the telecasting of NBA basketball games throughout the country. Through the years, we went "two by two" from Toledo to Tashkent and from Dayton to Dubai— wherever our business took us.

Jesus established the "two by two" *modus operandi* with His disciples, and, as you might expect, it worked beautifully. Scripture records that the disciples' success working "two by two" brought joy to Jesus, and He praised His Father for the effectiveness of His men. The effectiveness of the "two by two" leadership style is further demonstrated in the building of the early church, during which pairs of dedicated workers spread the Gospel and built the greatest organization of all time.

The leadership lesson is obvious: in almost every endeavor, the "two by two" system is the method to use, particularly when sending young people into a new territory for the first time; they will both learn and accomplish more together than they would individually.

CHAPTER 45

MISINFORMATION
MARK 6:14–29

King Herod heard about this,

for Jesus' name had become well known.

Mark 6:14

This passage illustrates that, in a fallen world, in spite of how well or how often we tell our story and how well we react to things said about us, there will always be those who "just don't get it," who don't understand. They may know our names, but they don't and *won't* know who we are. This is not a reason to give up our publicity or public relations efforts, but, instead, it is a challenge to continue the work in hopes that some *will* "get it," some *will* understand.

Jesus' name had become well known, but even the king did not know who He really was. Others speculated wildly about who He might be, and both John the Baptist and Jesus Himself told the people who He was, but many really didn't want to hear or understand.

This is a lesson leaders need to fully comprehend, illustrating yet another cost of leadership. And the greater the success of leadership, the more misunderstanding and misinformation there will be, much of it personal. Just think of Jesus' own experience. He was and is the greatest leader of all time, performing many more miracles than were recorded in the Gospels; for more than two thousand years He has changed lives, inspiring men and women to do good. His Holy Spirit ministers to millions every day. To say the least, His name has "become well known." But still so many do not know *Him*, failing to understand who *He* really is. There is still much wild speculation about Him, even though we have the Bible—the greatest good news account of all time—and the Holy Spirit, an even greater teacher than John the Baptist.

As a leader, many may know your name. Few will know who you *really* are.

CHAPTER 46

FACING
A LOSS

She went out and said

to her mother, "What shall I ask for?"

"The head of John the Baptist," she answered.

Mark 6:24

Think of how Jesus must have felt when John the Baptist was imprisoned and then executed in such a horrible way.

Jesus knew, of course, that all of John's trouble—and ultimately his death—was directly related to His own mission. Jesus praised John as he did no other human, exposing the very special bond between them. Think of how that bond must have strengthened as

John baptized Jesus, witnessing the blessing Jesus received from God the Father.

We know from Matthew that John's own disciples told Jesus of His death, the sad news driving Him to withdraw "by boat privately to a solitary place." But He had little time and little chance to mourn; the crowds came and, even in His time of grief for His fallen follower, Jesus had compassion on them and began to teach. A follower—the greatest of all followers—was lost, but the mission went on. The leader had little time to grieve, in no way indicating any callousness or lack of feeling on Jesus' part. His heart must have been broken, but His compassion for the living and the importance of His mission pushed Him on.

In analyzing our ability and willingness to lead, this sad episode in the life of Jesus provides another good test. Depending upon the importance of the enterprise, are you willing to continue to lead, to move ahead and focus on the future of the mission, even in the face of the loss of a devoted follower?

CHAPTER 47

VISIBLE LEADERSHIP

The apostles gathered around Jesus

and reported to him all

they had done and taught.

Mark 6:30

Many people have forgotten that the original owner of the Miami Dolphins—the great NFL franchise—was Danny Thomas, the wonderful entertainer and humanitarian. Many of us who joined in the effort to build the franchise were attracted to the enterprise by the opportunity to work for him. The Atlanta Falcons came into existence the same year, but for me the Dolphins were more appealing because of Danny Thomas.

Danny lived in Hollywood and only came to Miami periodically. When he did, it was an exciting time for those who constituted the Dolphins' first office staff. We were eager to report to him all that we were doing to build the team and franchise; however, he was sometimes too busy to see all of us during his brief visit, and, thirty years later, I still remember how disappointed I was when he was unable to meet with me. He was my leader, and I wanted to report to him.

As you lead, the idea to have your people report to you in written form may seem to be a good one: you can peruse the reports as you have the time to do so; you have a written record of your workers' activities; and you are able to jot appropriate notes back—all very neat and orderly, but so much is lost. A wise leader does not rely solely on notes and memos to communicate with those he leads; he makes certain to allow for time to "lead by walking around" (to use a Tom Peters phrase). He or she sees and is seen by those doing the work, and this is important so that team members can receive regular personal time from and easy access to their leader whenever necessary.

When His disciples returned from the successful mission on which Jesus sent them, one which enabled them to practice many of the things He had told them, can you imagine how eager they were to report to Him? This must have been a joyful, energizing time.

As you lead, don't waste valuable opportunities to lead by saying, "Just send me a note on that." Take Jesus' lead—gather your people around you and let them tell you "all they [have] done and taught."

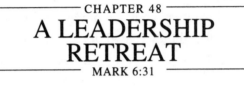

——— CHAPTER 48 ———
A LEADERSHIP
RETREAT
——— MARK 6:31 ———

Then, because so many people were coming

and going that they did not even have a chance to eat,

he said to them, "Come with me by yourselves

to a quiet place and get some rest."

Mark 6:31

In the above verse, Jesus lays out all the directions necessary for a productive leadership retreat—corporate, church, or family.

During more than forty years in business, I have been to my share of leadership retreats, the most productive of which followed the simple guidelines laid down for us by Jesus. When we deviated from those, our company retreats were less productive than they might have been.

One of the temptations we sometimes find hard to resist is planning a retreat that allows time to "get a little work done." This sounds like a contradiction in terms—a retreat where work is done—but at our corporate retreats and at Christian college board retreats, there is often some work built into the agenda, usually a mistake. Jesus said, "Get some rest," which should be the primary purpose of a retreat.

We scheduled several past retreats in a big city or a theme park setting as a way of rewarding our employees. *Big* mistake. It is sometimes productive to reward *individual* employees and their families with a trip, but a retreat should be like the one Jesus proposed for His disciples—in a "quiet place."

Another common mistake is to bring in numerous speakers to a corporate retreat setting. Certainly there is a time for consultants, outside experts, and inspirational speakers. However, every enterprise should have at least one yearly retreat to which the leader's invitation should say, "Come with me by yourselves." A wise leader will always schedule time with followers that excludes outsiders. These are times of great importance and significance and should not be missed.

CHAPTER 49

CAPTURING UNPLANNED MOMENTS

MARK 6:30–34

When Jesus landed and saw a large crowd,

he had compassion on them,

because they were like sheep without a shepherd.

So he began teaching them many things.

Mark 6:34

Wise leaders will always have a schedule, a plan to use time most productively, but the wisest leader will never make it his master.

Important but unplanned moments periodically occur that should not be lost, even though they disrupt a planned schedule. One of the tensions of leadership is finding the proper balance between adhering to a well-planned schedule and being flexible enough not to lose those spontaneous opportunities that cross our paths. This is not easy. I have seen both extremes.

Some leaders seem to careen from one unplanned event to another, their schedules meaning nothing. I know of one corporation chairman whose company has been severely damaged because of his failure to keep any sort of schedule, resulting in broken relationships, severed alliances, and lost business opportunities. At the other extreme, I have seen leaders who rarely deviated from a planned schedule, resulting in many missed opportunities. Both extremes are examples of ineffective leadership.

How do we find a balance? Jesus had a plan, one which He moved inexorably to accomplish. But as He did so, He utilized those special, unplanned occasions to contribute to the successful conclusion of His original plan. By following a schedule until and unless those special opportunities arise that will make the overall goal more attainable, you will maintain a schedule that works for you and your organization.

As in the above passage, compassion was typically Jesus' motivation for deviating from His schedule.

Compassion may not seem useful for today's leaders in intense business situations, but consider this: a concern for the welfare of people rarely leads us to an unprofitable or unproductive use of our time. Wise compassion, the kind that moved Jesus, does not cause a leader to become so weak that he damages the enterprise or hurts those around him. Rather, it is a clearheaded emotion that enables us to strive to accomplish the most good for the most people. Sometimes this is achieved by closely adhering to a schedule. Sometimes it is achieved by being flexible and taking compassionate detours that help to accomplish your overall goal.

When thinking about your schedule, remember how Jesus approached His.

CHAPTER 50

BOLDNESS
BUILDS
LEADERSHIP
MARK 6:35–44

But he answered,

"You give them something to eat."

Mark 6:37

Boldness builds leadership, but rashness destroys it. Discerning between the two is critical.

My life and business career have been blessed by associations with bold leaders. Among those, David F. Dixon stands out as perhaps the boldest. I can still remember when he said, "Bob, we are going to build the world's greatest stadium, and we are going to build it in downtown New Orleans."

Sure, Dave. I ticked off the problems in my head. Louisiana is an unlikely place for the world's largest stadium. New Orleans is among the smallest television markets. And to top it off, I knew that voters in the northern part of the state rarely supported projects in New Orleans. The whole idea seemed far fetched to me. None of that deterred Dave Dixon from following through with his vision, and the Superdome in New Orleans stands as a monument to his boldness while it continues to serve the people of Louisiana.

When Jesus told the disciples to feed the five thousand, it was among His boldest leadership moves, but it wasn't rash. He knew He could make it happen; it was His shortsighted disciples who saw only the crowds but forgot about their Master, who had already worked miracles far more amazing than feeding a few thousand hungry people (which is harder: feeding the hungry or raising the dead?).

By saying "You feed them," Jesus did three things every leader must do at some point: (1) He imparted a vision that only He could see; (2) He delegated full authority to His subordinates to accomplish the task at hand; and (3) He allowed them to share fully in the fulfillment of the vision.

When Dave Dixon told me that we were going to build a great domed stadium in downtown New Orleans, it was also a bold—not a rash—statement, one that reflected a bold vision. Although he certainly did not have the perfect foresight of Jesus, Dave "knew" we were going to build the stadium. This kind of knowledge is called leadership—*bold* leadership.

In the home, in our churches, in business, and in education, people thirst for bold leadership. People follow bold leaders, eventually becoming bold themselves. The feeding of the five thousand contributed to the boldness ultimately displayed by the disciples as they faced and conquered every obstacle they encountered in their quest to spread the gospel. The benefits of bold leadership continue even after the leader has disappeared from the scene.

Jesus is the greatest and boldest of all leaders. His followers, particularly those in positions of leadership today, need to view boldness as the norm, not as an elusive, extraordinary leadership style. Again, boldness is not rashness or cockiness. Bold leadership, the kind Jesus practiced, dares great things with great faith to accomplish great good.

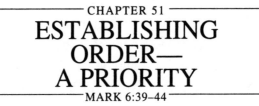

CHAPTER 51

ESTABLISHING ORDER— A PRIORITY

——————— MARK 6:39–44 ———————

Then Jesus directed them to have all the people

sit down in groups on the green grass.

Mark 6:39

One of a leader's first responsibilities is to establish order.

We serve a God of order. A significant function of His act of Creation was to bring order out of chaos. Before Jesus fed the five thousand, He instructed the disciples to organize the crowd. In fact, His compassion for them was triggered by their lack of order: "They were like sheep without a shepherd."

Moving into any situation, an effective leader begins by creating order. Don't mistake a martinet for a leader. A martinet does create order, but only for the sense of power and control it gives him. A leader creates order so he or she can more effectively serve others. Jesus encouraged the people to sit in groups so that He and the disciples could better serve them. For a leader, order is never merely an exercise of power, but a necessary part of preparation for service.

Contrary to popular opinion, order does not stifle creativity, but promotes it. It does not restrict freedom, but enhances it for the greatest number. Disorder is a kind of tyranny in which good things seldom happen. When disorder reigns, people suffer in many ways.

There is a vast difference between order and regimentation. Jesus didn't tell the five thousand to sit down in groups, organized alphabetically by last name, to count off, and remain silent until addressed. Instead, He created an order that was not ominous and restrictive, but pleasant and liberating. Regimentation stifles creativity and restricts freedom, but order creates an environment where freedom and creativity flourish.

CHAPTER 52

LEADERS PRAY IN GRATITUDE

MARK 6:45–52

After leaving them,

he went up on a mountainside to pray.

Mark 6:46

This short passage of only seven verses contains many leadership lessons, the key one being that prayer is as necessary after triumph as it is before difficulty.

Our tendency is to pray when facing peril, but to forget prayer after God has seen us through hard times. Jesus prayed before feeding the five thousand as He gave thanks for the bread; but even more significantly, *after* the great miracle and *after* dismissing the crowd and sending His disciples away, "he went up on a mountainside to pray." This is a great lesson for everyone who leads.

Time alone, time in *prayer* alone, is necessary for successful leadership. Certainly, prayer is important as we look toward the inevitable difficulties we will face, but Jesus shows us that it is also vital *after* God has allowed our leadership to succeed. These times of prayer strengthen and sustain us—perhaps more than any other—and should be the most joyful and memorable times of praise, worship, and celebration of our wonderful heavenly Father; times for thanks and thanksgiving, and times of expressing love and adoration. The only petitioning in these times of prayer should be for the grace to love Him more.

After He has seen us—or allowed us to lead others—through difficulty, we should be certain to go to Him in prayer. This is not a time for casual prayer that we whisper as we move on to our next activity. Jesus could easily have gone with His disciples as they left for Bethsaida, which would have been the natural, expected thing to do. Why wait and travel alone? Because God's great help and great blessing demanded a particularly meaningful time of communion with Him.

Ingratitude displeases God. In Old Testament times, the ungratefulness of the children of Israel frequently provoked God to anger. Their leader, Moses, often had to intercede on their behalf.

As a leader today, with the knowledge of the scriptural account, the great joy of knowing Jesus, and access to the help of the Holy Spirit, it is even more important that we express our thanks after times of help, blessing, and triumph. Doing this will allow us to approach our Father more confidently when we again need His help in facing a difficult situation. How can we go to Him with another petition when we did not thank Him or worship Him when He first provided for us?

The best leaders are also the most thankful people on earth because they realize that everything they have is a gift from God. Be thankful and remember the One from whom all blessings flow.

David's expression in Psalm 138:1–3 should be a pattern for leaders and is an appropriate way to close our book on the leadership lessons of Jesus:

I will praise you, O LORD, with all my heart;
before the "gods" I will sing your praise.
I will bow down before your holy temple

and will praise your name
for your love and your faithfulness,
for you have exalted above all things
your name and your word.
When I called, you answered me;
you made me bold and stouthearted.

God bless you as you lead in your home, church, and business. Continue to look to Jesus, our ultimate leader.

MORE
LEADERSHIP
LESSONS
OF
JESUS

This book is dedicated to Dr. Robert S. Folsom,
who has demonstrated the leadership lessons of Jesus
in sports, business, public service, and philanthropy.
I am grateful for his leadership in my life.
—Bob Briner

This book is dedicated to John and Helen Sergey,
missionaries for sixty years to the people of Russia.
—Ray Pritchard

TABLE OF CONTENTS

ACKNOWLEDGMENTS

Once again, Dr. Ray Pritchard has proven to be an extraordinary writing partner. It is a joy to acknowledge, not only his major contribution to our joint writing effort, but also his contributions to my life as a friend, mentor, and spiritual guide.

Too, my wife Marty continues to be both inspiration and solid practical help in all I do. This certainly includes the writing of this book. I am grateful.

Jennifer Heldman has been a most faithful assistant, and I am appreciative.

Bob Briner

My friendship with Bob Briner is one of the great joys of my life. I am honored to partner with him once again. When people ask how I can pastor a church and write books at the same time, I tell them that I couldn't do it without the men and women who serve with me on staff. I am indebted to Kathy Duggins, Mia Gale, Sherrie Puknaitis, Phyllis Raad, and Cindy Todd for many kindnesses, large and small. They take care of many details and help keep my life organized. Special thanks to wife Marlene—my best friend and the person I trust more than anyone in the world. Nothing I do would be possible without her support. I pray for my three sons—Joshua, Mark, and Nicholas—that they might someday become men of God who lead as Jesus did.

Ray Pritchard

INTRODUCTION

He died well before His fortieth birthday. He never traveled more than 100 miles from His birthplace. His public ministry lasted less than four years. He left behind a handful of followers and told them to change the world.

They did. Twenty centuries have come and gone and the world is still changed because of what they did after He left.

When all the facts are fairly considered, we may safely say that Jesus Christ is the most effective leader the world has ever known. The tiny band He left behind has now become a worldwide fellowship numbering nearly two billion people in every nation on every continent.

How did He do it? We believe the Bible answers that question. This book is the second volume we have written on the leadership lessons of Jesus. The first volume covered the story of Jesus from the Gospel of Mark, chapters 1–6. This volume picks up the narrative at chapter 7 and carries it through chapter 10. As you turn the pages, you will follow Jesus as He moves slowly toward His date with destiny in

Jerusalem. Along the way you will discover how He took a group of very unlikely men and molded them into leaders who would carry on His work after He returned to heaven. You will have a front-row seat to some of the most amazing miracles ever recorded. After two thousand years no one can say how Jesus healed a blind man or fed four thousand people with only seven loaves of bread. We only know that He did it because He was and is the Son of God from heaven.

Keep reading and you will listen in as Jesus goes one-on-one with His harshest critics. These clashes with people in authority teach us much about how to respond to criticism without losing our sense of mission.

A few chapters later Jesus takes His disciples on a retreat to a place called Caesarea Philippi. There He challenges them to declare their personal commitment to Him and His mission. From that moment on He begins to speak openly to them about His coming death. This episode teaches us much about communicating our vision to our key associates and the importance of time and place in asking for a personal commitment.

In the last few chapters Jesus seems to be everywhere at once—healing a boy with an evil spirit, then settling a dispute among the disciples, then answering questions about divorce, and finally spending important one-on-one time with the man known as the rich young ruler. Our journey ends as Jesus travels the last few miles from Jericho to Jerusalem, healing a blind man along the way.

INTRODUCTION

We hope you will catch a glimpse of the most important Person ever to walk on planet earth. If you have dismissed Jesus as an irrelevant religious figure, think again. The Jesus you will meet in these pages is not some dim, distant icon. He is the Son of God and the greatest leader history has ever known. After twenty centuries His message still speaks to modern men and women.

We have intentionally kept each chapter short because we know how busy life is for most people. If you have a Bible handy, please take time to read the corresponding passages from Mark. By doing that you will gain much more from our comments and application.

Feel free to take your time reading this book. As authors, we won't mind if you underline sentences you like or make notes in the margin. Jot down questions that come to your mind. Take what we have written and apply it to your situation. Add your own comments. May this book inspire you to become a leader like Jesus.

Now we're ready to begin. Let's roll back the clock two thousand years and join Jesus and His disciples as unexpected visitors interrupt a pleasant meal. If you're ready, we now join a story in progress as Jesus teaches us how to deal with our critics.

CHAPTER 1

HOW TO HANDLE OPPOSITION

MARK 7:1–7

The Pharisees and some of the teachers of the law who had come from

Jerusalem gathered around Jesus and saw some of his disciples eating

food with hands that were "unclean," that is, unwashed.

Mark 7:1

Leaders have a constant companion. It is opposition. If you lead, you *will* have those who oppose you. Be ready with answers for your critics, and do not let unjust or unwarranted criticism discourage you. (It is very important to be able to discern the difference between unjust or unwarranted criticism and constructive criticism given by caring friends, which is valuable to every leader.)

Opposition will often come in the form of attacks on your people, as was the case in the passage cited above. The Pharisees sought to distract and disrupt Jesus by attacking His disciples. Make no mistake about it—an attack on your followers is an attack on your leadership. As you defend your followers, you do two things. First, you defend yourself. Second, as your followers see you standing up for them, their loyalty to you and to your leadership is greatly enhanced.

While it is important to defend and speak up for your followers in public, this does not mean that you turn a blind eye to their actions that need reproof and correction. Followers *do* make mistakes. Some mistakes are honest. But some followers use their position to do bad things. Both need correction; the latter needs rebuke. In almost every circumstance, a leader will be wise to correct or rebuke followers in private or at least within an inner circle.

Note the way Jesus rebuked the disciples and the circumstances throughout the Gospels in which He did it. Jesus did not directly answer the criticism of the Pharisees, nor did He directly criticize their man-made rules. Instead, He dealt with the heart of the issue—man-made rules versus God's eternal law.

Nothing in this passage suggests that the Pharisees were wrong to establish certain traditions regarding ceremonial washings. Those traditions were meant to remind the Jews of their inner uncleanness and the absolute necessity of approaching God with a clean heart. But somehow that noble purpose had been twisted into an extrabiblical standard for judging others. When Jesus called them "hypocrites," it wasn't because of their rules, but because of their judgmental spirit that contradicted the very point of hand washing in the first place.

Jesus (1) responded to unjust criticism, (2) defended His disciples, and at the same time (3) refocused the issue away from His followers and back on His critics. Jesus did a masterful job of showing how a leader handles his critics without getting unnecessarily sidetracked.

CHAPTER 2

DEFINING YOUR MISSION STATEMENT

"You have let go of the commands of God and are holding

on to the traditions of men."

Mark 7:8

Effective leaders see beyond the traditional way of doing things and look for better ways. They do this, however, realizing that some things are sacrosanct, and they always keep the ultimate goal in mind. This is why it is so important to have a well-thought-out, closely defined, easily understood mission statement. Without this, even the most compelling and charismatic leaders get off track and go astray. A mission statement to which reference is constantly made is essential to quality leadership. Without this, personality, pride, and the exigencies of the moment will be diverting.

For Jesus, "the commands of God," doing His Father's will, constituted His mission statement. The "traditions of men" were never going to sidetrack Him from His goal. He was not to be diverted.

Again, the point to notice in verse 8 is *not* that the Pharisees were "holding on" to the traditions of men. We all do that to some extent because tradition helps us take the best of the past as a guide while we walk into the future. Jesus might be wrongly seen here as attacking all tradition. Instead, He excoriates the Pharisees for having "let go" of the commands of God. When you place your own traditions underneath God's will, they serve as a positive guide. But when the order is reversed, you end up exactly like the Pharisees—abandoning God's will for your personal agenda.

Note the specific example Jesus gives in verses 9–13. Evidently some Pharisees were using this man-made tradition of "Corban" to evade the clear teaching of Scripture to care for their parents. In light of the Fifth Commandment, this was a truly evil thing to do. First Timothy 5:8 reminds us that a believer who doesn't care for his own family is actually worse than an unbeliever. Christian leaders must never use their calling in business as an excuse to neglect their loved ones.

In a real sense, leaders of today have the same general mission statement. God's will should be the overall mission statement of every leader. Under this umbrella, our more personal mission needs to be spelled out specifically. An effective leader will understand his mission, be able to articulate it, and keep both himself and his followers from getting diverted. Vision, mission, and strategy are all necessary for quality leadership.

Be sure you have a mission statement for your life as well as for every leadership effort you undertake.

CHAPTER 3

CALLING THE CROWD

Again Jesus called the crowd to him and said,

"Listen to me, everyone, and understand this."

Mark 7:14

Words, at least as much as actions, are the tools of leadership and have awesome power. Great leaders throughout history have won significant victories by what they said and when they said it, and their words live long after most of their actions are forgotten.

Our key verse tells us that Jesus "called the crowd to him." There are times when leaders should not wait for an opportunity to speak; they should create one. When there are misunderstandings, when the opposition is getting its message out, when morale is low, or when morale is high are times when a leader will do well to call the crowd to himself.

Historians say that John F. Kennedy won the U.S. presidency by just such a calling of a crowd to himself. Kennedy, a Roman Catholic, spoke to a group of Protestant clergymen in Houston, Texas, and by his words defused most of their opposition to his candidacy. After this speech, his religion was never much of a factor in the election. His very narrow margin of victory points to the importance of one speech.

In that famous Houston speech Kennedy calmed the fears of the clergymen by professing his devotion to the Constitution of the United States and by appealing to the First Amendment guarantee of freedom of religion. His speech was effective because he (1) ventured into a potentially hostile audience, (2) faced the problem head-on, (3) appealed to common ground, and (4) in so doing, spoke through that audience to an entire nation.

About one hundred years earlier, another U.S. president delivered a speech that stirred the nation in Gettysburg, Pennsylvania. Abraham Lincoln, with only a few well-chosen words, actually reshaped American history and redefined the dream of democratic government. The Gettysburg Address is still widely quoted and beloved. Great speeches need not be long, but they must be thoughtfully prepared, timely, and spoken with forthright courage.

When a leader calls a crowd, the stakes go up. Be sure the time is right, and be sure you have something important to say. Don't become so mesmerized by your own oratorical powers that you overuse them. On the rare occasions when you do call people to you, your message must be both cogent and compelling.

Today, far too often, leaders neglect doing the hard work of learning to speak well. This is a big mistake. Even in our high-tech world, there will be times when a great, timely oral presentation will pay huge dividends. In some instances it can be the difference between success or failure. Be ready for occasions when your words will reveal the essence of your leadership.

CHAPTER 4

GUARD YOUR HEART
MARK 7:14–23

"Nothing outside a man can make him 'unclean' by going into him.

Rather, it is what comes out of a man that makes him 'unclean.'"

Mark 7:15

In light of verses 14–23, Jesus is challenging these religious leaders to consider the condition of their own hearts. It's easy to judge others as long as you don't look at yourself first. But judging will take on a different hue when you remember that you are not as good as you think you are. Jesus' whole point is: Don't sweat the food you eat—whether it is "clean" or "unclean"—because sin lurks inside you regardless of your diet or whether or not you washed your hands. *An effective leader guards his own heart because everything important in life comes from the inside out.*

Proverbs 4:23 states Jesus' point well: "Above all else, guard your heart, for it is the wellspring of life." The term *heart* in the Bible generally refers to the innermost part of life. It is the decision-making center, the source of motives, the seat of the passions, and the center of the conscience. It is truly the place "where life makes up its mind."

Proverbs has a great deal to say about the heart. It is the source of wisdom (2:10) and understanding (8:5), the origin of both deceit (6:14) and joy (15:30). The heart may backslide (14:14) or trust in God (3:5). It may be cheerful (15:13), prideful (16:5), bitter (14:10), haughty (18:12), or prudent (18:15). The heart may lust after an adulterous woman (6:25), it may rage against the Lord (19:3), and it may eventually be hardened against God altogether (28:14). The Lord tests the heart (17:3) because He knows what is in it (24:12), which is why the heart must be guarded all the time (4:23).

Jesus almost certainly had this verse in mind when He spoke to the Pharisees in Matthew 12:34b: "For out of the overflow of the heart the mouth speaks." This verse cuts both ways. Whatever is on the inside will eventually come out— whether good or bad. If a person's heart is dirty, he cannot produce purity in his life. Likewise, if the heart is stayed on the Lord, it will be seen on the outside eventually. The King James Version of Proverbs 23:7 reads, "As [a man] thinketh in his heart, so is he."

If you think angry thoughts, angry words are sure to follow.

If you fill your mind with sexual fantasies, your body will find a way to fulfill those desires.

If you dwell on your problems, they will soon overwhelm you.

If you feel like a victim, soon you will become one.

If you give way to worry, don't be surprised when you get ulcers.

If you focus on how others misunderstand you, you will soon become angry and bitter.

What goes in must come out. Sooner or later your thoughts translate into reality. You're not what you think you are; but what you think, you are. The flip side is also true.

If you focus on the truth, you will speak the truth.

If you look on noble things, nobility will mark your life.

If you seek out lovely things, your life will be lovely to others.

If you dwell on the right, the wrong will seem less attractive to you.

If you look for virtue, you will find it.

If you search for higher things, you will elevate your own life.

Recently a friend sent me this prayer from the *Book of Common Prayer*. It seems a fitting way to apply the words of Proverbs 4:23: "Almighty God, to you all hearts are open, all desires known, and from you no secrets are hid: Cleanse the thoughts of our hearts by the inspiration of your Holy Spirit, that we may perfectly love you and worthily magnify your Holy Name; through Christ our Lord. Amen."

CHAPTER 5

THE POWER OF A REBUKE

"Are you so dull?" he asked.

Mark 7:18

This passage is full of leadership lessons. The overriding one is that sometimes a sharp rebuke is a necessary and productive leadership tool. Jesus was no Milquetoast, namby-pamby leader. On several occasions He was exasperated with His disciples and let them know about it in no uncertain terms. In today's language He said, "Will you guys wake up? Aren't you ever going to get it? How many times do I have to explain it to you?" Those you lead will sometimes need to know you are not happy with them.

Note also the brevity of the question—"Are you so dull?" No doubt that stung. Just one quick question, then on to an explanation—perhaps with a bit of a sigh that He had to cover the same ground once more. *Wise leaders wait for the right moment, give a sharp rebuke, and then move on.* Foolish leaders keep repeating their criticisms endlessly, which leads not to better performance but to resentment and discouragement.

Good leaders use rebukes, especially the stinging ones, sparingly and strategically. They never use them to tear down or to ridicule for the sake of ridiculing. They always have a positive purpose. That purpose should never be to show how macho or clever the leader is or to give the leader ego gratification. Rebukes should hurt the leader as much as the one being rebuked.

One corporate leader always seemed to need a "punching bag," a person to be the target of his ridicule. Over a number of years, he "used up" many talented men and women, people he would bring into his inner circle and then subject to such constant and vitriolic ridicule that they would eventually move on, to be replaced by another object of his scorn. (The happy corollary to this is that several of these people went on to become very successful, even at a national level. But because of the incessant, unfair ridicule, their talents were lost to the original company.)

Note that the disciples' rebuke took place "away from the crowd." That is, Jesus didn't upbraid His disciples in front of the onlookers. In fact, He not only waited until they were in private, but He also waited until the question came from them. That way it would not seem as if He were out to get them or to humiliate them.

Timing is everything—both in giving compliments and criticisms. Jesus didn't hesitate to challenge His followers when He felt they weren't paying enough attention to what He was saying and doing. But He always did it in a way that preserved their dignity even while driving the painful point home.

Also note that the rebuke didn't involve what they didn't know, but rather what they should have known. It doesn't do any good to chastise your workers for failure to achieve goals that have never been explained to them.

Obviously, Jesus never made this kind of mistake. His rebukes were always for both the good of the person and the success of the enterprise. His example shows that a carefully considered rebuke, given with positive results in mind, is a leadership tool not to be neglected.

CHAPTER 6

JESUS' GLOBAL PLAN
MARK 7:24–26

Jesus left that place and went to the vicinity of Tyre.

Mark 7:24a

Tyre and Sidon were well-known centers of pagan culture in Jesus' day. They were commercial seaports on the eastern shore of the Mediterranean Sea that attracted traders from throughout the ancient world. The people of these cities were sophisticated, well educated, and deeply immersed in Greek culture, all of which was apparent in the many beautiful buildings, including elaborate temples dedicated to various heathen deities.

Is it perhaps significant that in the immediately preceding passage (7:14–23), Jesus speaks to the disciples about the importance of inner purity? His message on the sins that come from the inside would keep them from hastily judging the Gentiles. And inner purity is always important, but especially when going into areas of life where you know temptation will stare you right in the face.

The amazing thing is, Jesus went there. He wasn't afraid to take His message to cities that others might consider "off-limits" or too evil to reach. Some of His disciples no doubt felt quite uneasy following Him to Tyre and Sidon. Most of them had probably never been there before and didn't want to ever be there again. However, going at this time prepared them for His later Great Commission to take the gospel to the ends of the earth.

Successful leaders have a plan that they pursue relentlessly. A significant part of Jesus' plan was to demonstrate that the gospel was not for the Jews only. Given the difficulty of travel, the compactness of the area in which He moved, and the social taboos against contacts with Gentiles, it is amazing how many contacts Jesus had with non-Jews during His brief earthly lifetime: with the Magi, who attended His birth; the Gadarenes; the Roman centurion; the Samaritan woman. Jesus met, interacted with, and ministered very productively to a wide variety of people. This is a powerful leadership lesson for today.

Given the constant "shrinking" of our planet and the influx of immigrants into American society, the wise leader will extend his or her leadership both to people beyond the borders and to people within, who come from a different cultural and ethnic background. It is an absolute necessity to plan with intentionality to interact productively with all the people of God's wonderful creation.

CHAPTER 7

THE STRATEGY OF SECRETS

He entered a house and did not want anyone to know it;

yet he could not keep his presence secret.

Mark 7:24b

A very basic—perhaps *the* most basic—tool of leadership is information. How, when, where, and to whom information is dispensed is the very substance of leadership. The passage quoted above provides a starting point for an understanding of a leader's handling of information. In a human sense, *even Jesus* could not keep something a secret, even though He wanted to do so.

A place to begin understanding information, then, is the fact of the extreme difficulty of keeping anything truly secret. For a leader to think that he or she can do anything with anonymity is folly. For a leader to think he or she can hide any dynamic information for very long is foolishness. As Benjamin Franklin said, "Three can keep a secret if two of them are dead."

Do not try to build a leadership based on secrecy. It may work for a time, but inevitably it breaks down. In years of corporate life, I observed some leaders who thought they could best lead by sharing confidences among subordinates who were then supposed to keep them private. In the end, this never worked, and what generally happened was that staff would begin comparing "confidences" and find that they were each told the same thing on what they thought was an exclusive basis. Even worse, they sometimes learned they were told things that were mutually exclusive and contradictory. Confidence in this kind of leadership quickly erodes. An open honest style of leadership is always best.

It is practically impossible to hold any sort of newsworthy announcement, good or bad, for very long. In today's world it will "leak." It is always much better for a leader to decide how to break the news in the most productive way at the *earliest possible moment*. Otherwise, you will almost always find yourself responding to it rather than controlling it.

The most successful "holding" operation in which I was personally involved still ended in a painful situation. When the great tennis star Arthur Ashe discovered he had contracted AIDS from a blood transfusion, a very small number of his closest friends covenanted with him to keep his affliction a secret until he would go public at a time of his choosing.

There were some things he wanted to accomplish before he faced the huge public clamor he knew would ensue.

This worked for several months, but inevitably, he was confronted with disclosure before he was ready. A team of us orchestrated the resulting tumultuous press conference as best we could, but it was still very painful for Arthur and his family.

A secret is very hard to keep. News is almost impossible to hold. A wise leader will remember this. Even Jesus could not keep things secret.

CHAPTER 8

SETTING LEADERSHIP PRIORITIES

MARK 7:26-30

"First let the children eat all they want," he told her, "for it is not right

to take the children's bread and toss it to their dogs."

Mark 7:27

To understand this passage, it is necessary to know that the "children" to whom Jesus refers are His disciples. As a leader with a plan, He knew He had to use every teachable moment to instruct His followers about the plan. He would be with them for only a limited time. He had to give them as much as possible if they were to be able to function without Him. The plan, its execution, and its longevity had to take priority.

A true leader understands that he or she will not always be with his or her followers. Such a leader's goal is to enable followers to function as well as possible in the absence of the leader, whether the absence is temporary or permanent. Good leaders discuss this openly and unself-consciously, as Jesus did. Shortsighted leaders build and execute a program based on the fallacy that they will always be there. Their program only works in an optimum way when they are present and the followers serve through the leader.

From the very beginning, Jesus set out to lead in such a way that His followers would be able to productively carry on without His physical presence. The plan worked brilliantly. The church is the evidence.

Just as it is important to know that the "children" in the passage are Jesus' disciples, it is also important to know that the "dogs" are everyone else. In using the term *dogs,* Jesus was not denigrating the woman. He was making a powerful statement about priorities. He was saying, in effect, that compared to His basic mission, everything else became of very little import. He knew the priorities. He was going to fulfill the plan.

By responding to the woman the way He does, Jesus is not only instructing His disciples about His primary mission; He is also testing her faith. What might seem an insult is actually a way of saying, "Do you know who I really am and why I came?" Get this: When she said, "Yes, Lord," that's the only time anyone directly calls Jesus "Lord" in the Gospel of Mark. Hmmm. And it comes—not from the disciples—but from a Gentile woman. Perhaps she sees things more clearly than some of His closest followers do.

Further, the whole incident serves as a preparation for the later Great Commission. He came as the Messiah of Israel, but also as the Savior of the world. There is a true sense in which Jesus and the woman understood something about His mission that His disciples had not yet figured out—that He had come ultimately for the people of the whole world.

The woman, in one of the most prescient statements in all of Scripture, makes the case that Jesus can help her without detracting from His plan. He can solve her problem, can perform an act of charity, without in any way weakening His essential cause. This is a powerful and important leadership lesson.

A few years ago *Newsweek* ran a remarkable article on business leadership. One aspect of the article listed ways to spot a leader in trouble—a leader who had stopped leading. It pointed out that one of the easiest ways to identify a leader in trouble is to note the number of outside boards and charitable activities in which he or she is involved. Excessive involvement in activities outside the principle endeavor indicates a leader who either can't face the difficulties within or has become bored or burned out. In either instance, the enterprise suffers.

This syndrome shows itself often in both the local church and in higher education. When a pastor accepts more and more outside speaking engagements and increasingly looks for areas of service away from the local church, his leadership is in trouble. Anyone in higher education could spend every day attending a worthwhile off-campus meeting. He or she could do some very good work on boards and commissions. But excessive involvement off campus indicates a serious leadership gap on campus.

Watch for this syndrome in your own leadership. Watch for it in leaders of enterprises important to you.

Jesus showed us that we should do acts of charity that do not keep us from performing our mission. As was the case with the woman whose daughter Jesus freed from demons, involvement in ancillary charitable activities can be beneficial to the primary goal. If in the context of giving the best possible effort in your leadership role, you have the opportunity to contribute to a charitable effort, you should do it. However, the *most charitable* thing a leader can do is to give priority to his or her area of primary leadership.

This story is rich with meaning for all of us. It is a lesson about priorities, a lesson about having a global vision, a lesson about faith, and a lesson about using seemingly "unplanned" events as important teaching tools.

CHAPTER 9

TIMING MATTERS

Then Jesus left the vicinity of Tyre and went through Sidon, down to the

Sea of Galilee and into the region of the Decapolis.

Mark 7:31

Jesus did not take the "normal" or expected route back from Tyre and Sidon. He seems to have gone east and then south through Decapolis, skirting the northern border of Galilee, His "home territory." Why? Two reasons.

First, His many miracles had caused a movement to arise to make Him king by force or acclamation—neither was part of His plan. Second, He also knew that there was rising opposition to His ministry among the Jewish leaders. Because He knew the time was not right to force a public confrontation, and because the crowds in Galilee didn't really understand who He was, He elected to temporarily bypass His "home territory" in favor of the Decapolis, cities which had previously been hostile to His message.

To understand the full leadership import of this Scripture, read Mark 5:17b–20: "Then the people began to plead with Jesus to leave their region. As Jesus was getting into the boat, the man who had been demon-possessed begged to go with him. Jesus did not let him, but said, 'Go home to your family and tell them how much the Lord has done for you, and how he has had mercy on you.' So the man went away and began to tell in the Decapolis how much Jesus had done for him. And all the people were amazed."

The last time Jesus had been in the Decapolis, the ten cities, the people had begged Him to leave. This time, evidently, they were happy to have Him there and begged Him to place His healing hand on their friend. What had changed? It seems obvious. Jesus had shown great wisdom and great leadership by forbidding the formerly demon-possessed man to accompany Him. Instead, by asking him to remain in his home region and to tell what Jesus had done for him, the man became a powerful and believable agent for the Lord. Jesus demonstrated that quality public relations based on truth and timely, well-directed publicity are valuable leadership techniques. He practiced both with great skill.

The two visits Jesus made to the Decapolis demonstrate some other basic leadership precepts. On His first visit the people asked Him to leave, and He did. He was wise enough to see that a proper foundation for His work had not yet been laid. Instead of trying to force Himself and His message on them, He left. But He left an important representative to prepare for His next visit.

When the time was right, He returned and ministered with great effect. What a lesson! A wise leader will not try to force his leadership on people who are not ready.

Strategic retreats are part of the smartest leadership. While a wise leader will not force his or her program, neither will a wise leader give up on a situation without allowing time and the laying of a better foundation to make the situation tenable. In our business of distributing sports television, we saw this principle work to good effect. In the 1970s Korea became a viable television market. We went there hoping to sell the Korean networks a major package of tennis events. However, the Koreans told us they had absolutely no interest in the sport of tennis and we should, in effect, get lost.

We left but continued to be in touch with them, showing them how well tennis worked on television in other Asian countries, particularly in Japan—a country they always try to emulate. Our patience and foundation-laying paid off in a big way, and Korea has become one of the best international markets for televised tennis, as well as other sports.

Important leadership lessons then are: (1) don't try to force your leadership or your program where there is not readiness for it; (2) use quality public relations and education to lay a good foundation; and (3) at the proper time, try again.

Remember both of Jesus' visits to the Decapolis and the leadership lessons they teach. Jesus never did anything haphazardly; even His "small" decisions always had a larger purpose behind them.

CHAPTER 10

STYLE, SUBSTANCE, AND SYMPATHY

MARK 7:33–35

After he took him aside, away from the crowd,

Jesus put his fingers into the man's ears.

Mark 7:33

In the passage cited above, the key phrase is "away from the crowd." As we survey the miracles of Jesus, we see that His miracles had two primary purposes. One was to perform an act of love and mercy for the recipient. The other was to advance the plan by teaching lessons important to the plan.

A leader needs both style and substance, but it is important to never put style over substance. The real, tangible results are what count the most. Jesus performed miracles as a completed work. Substance. He also paid great attention to the "style" in which the miracles were performed. But even in paying attention to style, He always resisted the "grandstand play." He never did anything for self-aggrandizement, but always to glorify the Father and to do the will of the One who sent Him. Both substance and style should advance the cause.

Today's leaders need to carefully consider the time and setting for announcements, product introductions, and demonstrations. Is the overall plan advanced better by pointing narrowly to close associates or by aiming broadly to influence a wider audience? The accomplishment of the primary goal should be the leader's focus.

Consider another important lesson Jesus teaches leaders in this passage. By touching the man's ears, Jesus shows His sympathy with the man. In the previous miracle, Jesus casts the demons out of the woman's daughter when she isn't even present. Here Jesus touches the ears, then touches the man's tongue with His own spittle—both very intimate, extremely personal gestures. Why? The first miracle shows His power to heal over a great distance, the second His intimate involvement with this man's suffering. Wise leaders recognize that not all decisions should be made in the same way, not all problems handled in an identical fashion.

Also, note that He sighed. An amazing statement—the only time such a thing happens and is recorded. He sighed—not out of the difficulty of the case, but in deep compassion with this man's suffering—and perhaps by extension for the suffering of the whole world. Remember, Mark never records an irrelevant detail. Here is proof that Jesus was "touched with the feeling of our infirmities."

Sometimes leaders must do things quickly and then move on. At other times they will stop, take their time, and by their actions and their words, demonstrate deep personal concern. There are no "rules" for when to do what—only the recognition that leadership demands different responses on different occasions.

When the president speaks from the Oval Office, he always wears a business suit and speaks with dignity. But when he visits the state fair he takes off his coat, sits down, and eats corn on the cob with the ordinary folks. Which picture makes the front page the next day? Unless he's declaring war, it's always the president with the people. In this passage full of good lessons for leaders, Jesus shows us more of His "human" side even while performing a mighty miracle.

CHAPTER 11

SETTING THE STANDARD
FOR EXCELLENCE

People were overwhelmed with amazement.

"He has done everything well," they said.

Mark 7:37

Jesus was, of course, the most amazing person who ever lived. He did everything better than anyone else ever has or ever will. He continues to do this as He "prepares a place for us," daily intercedes on our behalf, and holds the world in place by the power of His Word.

We can never hope to overwhelm and amaze others the way He did, with His greatness and power. For leaders of today, however, the good news is that it takes relatively little to overwhelm and amaze. Our society has grown so far away from the standards Jesus set that today's leaders can stand out in stark and positive contrast to those around them by doing even the small things well. And doing the small things well is the basis for doing the big things well—the basis for quality, effective leadership.

Leaders used to lead by both precept *and* example, beginning with the small things. There are CEOs whose companies have high-sounding and noble mission statements, but whose own conduct and deportment in the small things is less than amazing or overwhelming. Unfortunately, the same kind of thing is often observable in churches. Some have a wonderful, expressive mission statement declaring that the intention of the church is to produce "caring servants"; but their staff, at the highest level of church leadership, fails to reflect that in the way they perform in the small, everyday interactions with people.

When a leader is always late, doesn't answer mail or return phone calls, or fails to say thanks, this is eventually reflected in the effectiveness of his or her leadership. Sooner or later, the enterprise suffers. These are small things, but they turn into big things. Fortunately, these are things all of us *can* do well. It only takes commitment and resolve. And if we, as leaders, will do these small things well, not only will our enterprise benefit, people will be overwhelmed with amazement because so few people bother these days.

Reflect on the truth of the parables of Jesus which teach that faithfulness in small things and trustworthiness in the seemingly mundane things of life lead to greater opportunities. Therefore, leaders who take care of the small things well in a small arena will most often have the opportunity to lead in a larger arena. Little things do mean a lot.

In Jesus' case, His overwhelming approval from the masses came because of His wisdom, His compassion, His sense of divine calling, and the unquestioned purity of His motives. It wasn't just His miracles, because even false prophets could work miracles (see Matt. 7:21–23). Miracles alone don't produce this kind of response.

We look at Jesus and think, "I could never perform the miracles He did." That's true, but any of us could—with the power He provides—live a life of giving and, in a small way at least, have a Christlike impact.

CHAPTER 12

MOMENTS OF COMPASSION

"I have compassion for these people; they have already been with me

three days and have nothing to eat."

Mark 8:2

Compassion is an absolute necessity for quality leadership. Without it, leadership becomes cold, self-serving, and tyrannical. The kind of leader who produces lasting, positive results, particularly results that last for eternity, *will* have compassion. If you do not genuinely care about those you lead and those you serve, get out of leadership. You will do more harm than good.

Here is a case where a leader acted wisely and with compassion simply because something needed to be done right then. Sometimes leaders do have to curtail their immediate plans in order to take care of those who follow them. For example, you might have to postpone a meeting, reschedule a trip, or come home early from vacation because of unforeseen problems among your workers. In such cases, the leader can either light a candle or "curse the darkness." Jesus used this opportunity to (1) meet the people's needs, (2) re-teach His disciples about His power to provide for His people, and (3) work an amazing miracle they would never forget. In so doing, He turned what could have been a disaster into a startling triumph.

There is a secondary lesson here as well. This is the second feeding miracle in Mark. The first one—recorded in Mark 6:30–44—happened in Israel and involved a mostly Jewish audience. This one happens in Decapolis and involves mostly Gentiles. Some critics have imagined that the Gospel writers for some reason invented two stories, but a cursory comparison shows many points of contrast.

Leaders shouldn't be surprised when the same problems crop up again and again. If you deal with big crowds of people in the desert, don't be surprised when they get hungry and thirsty.

Sometimes leaders complain or act surprised when problems recur, sometimes with different audiences. It's not always a sign of bad planning that problems repeat themselves.

Jesus doesn't appear bothered or flustered in this passage any more than in the earlier one. He simply sees the need and moves to meet the need. What a simple lesson, but how much we need it!

CHAPTER 13

KNOW YOUR RESOURCES

"How many loaves do you have?" Jesus asked. "Seven," they replied.

Mark 8:5

An effective leader knows the extent of his resources. He is willing to ask the necessary questions in order to know. He doesn't rely on guesswork. He gets the numbers from the ones who know.

Obviously, Jesus knew the answer to the question before He even asked. Just as obviously, He wanted to involve His disciples in the situation and make them a part of the undertaking to solve the problem. He could, of course, have handled everything with just a divine word. By not doing it this way, He provided leadership lessons for His disciples and for us as well.

Historians tell us that General Robert E. Lee constantly asked his subordinates — even on the very day of his surrender at Appomattox—"What opportunities do we have before us?" He did this (1) in order that he might not miss any strategic possibilities, and (2) to train his officers to see the larger picture. When Jesus asked the disciples how many loaves they had, He immediately involved them in the solution to the problem at hand. Good leaders must know what they have, and they must train their followers to start with whatever they have on hand.

A wise leader looks for ways to involve those he leads in as many productive activities as possible. A leader's job is not to do, but to get things done. A wise leader will resist the impulse to do things himself in favor of allowing his followers to learn and grow by doing it. A leader should, to the extent possible, do *only* those things which *only* he or she can do. The other things should be delegated.

When a leader becomes involved in doing nonleadership things, except for the purpose of teaching, the enterprise suffers. A leader's time should be devoted to planning and meeting the overall needs of the organization, delegating, inspiring, motivating, and teaching. Allow others to grow by allowing them to learn by doing.

In this story Jesus, the leader, sees the need and decides that He must meet it. He then expresses His commitment, which His followers think is futile. He surveys their resources, divides the crowd, performs the miracles, uses His disciples to serve the food, and later uses them to clean up afterwards. In short, Jesus here does what only He can do—

a miracle—and involves His disciples in every other part of the event. That's truly good leadership.

Note that Jesus was not offended or angered by their doubt. He knew that doubt could become a wonderful teaching tool. Seen in purely human terms, their paltry resources were nothing against the overwhelming need. But they had evidently forgotten the earlier miracle or doubted Jesus could do it again, perhaps thought that He wouldn't do it again in Gentile territory. In any case, leaders must be prepared for doubt and skepticism from within the inner circle. Such a moment provides a supreme test of the leader's vision . . . and his self-control. If he loses his cool, he loses their respect and also the chance to show them how a leader reacts wisely under pressure.

Jesus, who could do all things well, made sure His disciples got the experience in doing things themselves. This would serve them and their vital enterprise well after Jesus was physically removed from their midst. This is a valuable lesson for all leaders.

CHAPTER 14

THE JOY OF ORDER

He told the crowd to sit down on the ground.

Mark 8:6a

Note the leadership principles in Mark 8:6:

1. *He* told the crowd: Personal leadership
2. He *told* the crowd: Clear instruction
3. He told *the crowd*: Mass communication
4. To sit down on the ground: Order out of chaos

Think about what would have happened if Jesus hadn't imposed order. There would have been a wild stampede as the food was handed out. Some would have gotten more than they needed while others would have gone hungry. A beautiful miracle would have been lost in the dust of a Middle Eastern food riot.

We serve a God of order. In the very act of creation, God brought order out of chaos. Jesus' leadership is characterized by the creation of order. Ours should be as well.

A leader's first responsibility is to bring about order. Without order, leadership is mundane and ineffective. Without order, planning is wasted. Leadership and order are inextricably intertwined.

It is important to realize that some people are gifted with an innate sense of order, and some are not. Leaders and potential leaders need to do an objective self-analysis about this area of their lives. Wise leaders and those who work with them will make sure that an otherwise gifted leader who lacks organizational skills will have the assistance of someone who is responsible for "picking up the pieces," making sure that order and orderliness are maintained.

This is particularly important in churches. Gifted pastor-teacher spiritual leaders are often not given to administration and to the orderly conduct of the church activities. In this sort of situation, it is vital that the senior pastor recognizes this and that someone is brought in as an administrative pastor to create and maintain order. The wise senior pastor will not resist this kind of help, but will welcome it and revel in it. An orderly context will make his other leadership gifts that much more effective for the kingdom. This is true in other fields as well, such as business and education. Do whatever it takes to eliminate any shortfalls in this area.

Sometimes leaders resist this because they feel insecure or somehow inadequate and tend to treat others as competitors and not team members. Sadly, they end up operating at 30 percent efficiency because they won't dare let anyone else "manage their weaknesses."

A home, particularly a Christian home, should be orderly. The leaders of the home, the father and the mother, should make order a high priority. Christian social psychologists tell us that disorder in the home robs us of a sense of joy. Without order, there can be no meaningful plan for the household to progress toward godliness.

Now, it is important to understand that order does not mean mindless regimentation enforced with martinet-like strictness. It does mean a neat, clean, and orderly residence, a reasonable schedule, obedient children, and considerate and loving adults. This kind of home produces and encourages leadership outside the home, advancing God's kingdom on two fronts. Fathers and mothers make an orderly home a priority. Leadership begins here.

To some people, taking the time to bring order out of chaos seems to be a heavy burden. "Just go with the flow." "Let the Spirit lead." "Don't worry about the details," they say. Yet in the end, the price of taking time to do things "decently and in order" is always lower than the price of letting things take their own course.

Our Heavenly Father is a God of order. Jesus' leadership is characterized by commitment to order. We must commit to it as well.

CHAPTER 15

BEGINNING WITH GRATITUDE

MARK 8:1–10

When he had taken the seven loaves and given thanks, he broke them and

gave them to his disciples to set before the people, and they did so.

Mark 8:6b

The resources of any leader are finite. Often they will seem inadequate for the situation. Jesus, who, of course, had infinite resources, teaches us in this passage that we are to be thankful for what we have and to use what we have in faith. Leaders are not to become paralyzed by the difficulty of circumstances.

Using what we have, with thanksgiving, and moving positively ahead in faith is often the beginning of a great leadership triumph. This is in no way advocating rash and foolish action; and as we have said before, strategic retreat is often the most positive thing we can do. The call here *is* for a leadership that will act, that will chip away at the problem with the resources at hand. Tom Peters calls this "Ready, fire, aim."

Many great and enduring enterprises, most great and enduring churches have begun with "seven loaves" and "a few small fish," resources totally inadequate for the situation. A visionary leader focused on what was at hand rather than on what wasn't, and began to build. Great things ensued. What often happens when we begin to use what we have is that others will be inspired to join and help. New resources are found and are brought to bear. In feeding the four thousand, God supplied. He still supplies needs, but most often responds to faith in action. When we move, He moves. A leader moves and directs his followers to move in a positive way. Doing nothing accomplishes nothing.

Don't miss the other vital leadership lesson in this passage. Jesus didn't wring His hands over the small supply and the enormity of the task; He gave thanks for the loaves and the fish. Why? Certainly to acknowledge that even the little that they had came from the gracious hand of God. Ungrateful leaders will never accomplish great things because ingratitude saps the soul of its creative strength. You can either sit around moaning about what you don't have, or you can give thanks and get to work with what you do have.

Note that after the feeding there were seven large baskets—a different word from the one used in Mark 6—containing leftovers. That is, there was more at the end than there was at the beginning—even after feeding four thousand men.

Thus it always is when leaders move to meet genuine needs, trusting in God, with grateful hearts, beginning where they are with the resources on hand. This kind of miracle happens in various ways every day as godly men and women do what Jesus did in the wilderness of Decapolis.

God blessed Jesus' supply and effort. Today He blesses those who take what they have, put it to work, and trust Him to make up whatever they lack.

CHAPTER 16

HANDLING CHALLENGES
TO YOUR LEADERSHIP
—————— MARK 8:11–13 ——————

The Pharisees came and began to question Jesus. To test him, they asked

for a sign from heaven.

Mark 8:11

Leaders will always be questioned and tested. I have known some leaders who feel that after they have demonstrated competence over time, they should be immune from challenging questions and testing. This is an unrealistic expectation. Unfortunately, people are never content with yesterday's brilliance, last week's good program, or last Sunday's wonderful sermon.

It is very instructive to note that the Pharisees began to question Jesus, test Him, and ask for a sign from heaven immediately after He had fed four thousand men with seven loaves and a few fish! By this time in His ministry,

Jesus had already done many other miraculous things in highly public settings. The word of these feats had spread far and wide. Still, the Pharisees questioned Him and wanted a sign from heaven.

Jesus knew that their motives weren't good and their request wasn't sincere. Their questioning was indeed a kind of trap meant to throw Jesus off course. Somehow they had managed to rationalize everything Jesus had already done. Either miracles were faked or staged, or perhaps they were just lucky coincidences. So now they asked for some showy demonstration. The implication was: If you do this, then we'll believe you. But in reality their minds were already made up.

Sometimes hearts can become so hardened that nothing we do or say can change them. Jesus recognized that, refused to argue, sighed deeply (one supposes, with a mixture of resignation and sadness), and moved on.

The best leaders can recognize the difference between legitimate questions and objections meant simply to throw you off track. One useful sign may be: If someone comes and asks you for "just one more" proof that your plan is going to work, think carefully before you offer that "one more" proof, lest you get caught in the trap of endlessly trying to please people who will never be pleased no matter what you do.

A dangerous and defeating response to this kind of questioning and testing is to say, "Okay, you want a sign? I'll give you a sign," and then to go out and do something that is not part of the plan and does not really further it, thinking it will silence the questioning critics. It never works. These kind of critics will not be silenced. It is much better to respond the way Jesus did—"sigh deeply" and move on.

As he often does, Billy Graham has much to teach us here. After a remarkable lifetime of humble dedicated service, after unprecedented success in preaching the gospel over many years, there are still those *within the church* who question him and test him. Dr. Graham almost never responds. He seems to "sigh deeply" and move on.

Dr. Graham relentlessly pursues his plan and his program. He is not distracted. He does not get in name-calling contests. He does not get defensive. He conducts another crusade. He preaches the gospel. What an example! It is a leadership lesson of Jesus, played out for us by a contemporary leader. We very much need to appropriate this lesson for our own leadership styles.

Never think you will escape questioning and testing. Based on your leadership record, the questioning and testing may be unfair and unwarranted. However, it will come. Be ready for it. Be ready to "sigh deeply" and move on with the plan God has called you to execute.

CHAPTER 17

A FLOATING SEMINAR

The disciples had forgotten to bring bread, except for one loaf they had

with them in the boat.

Mark 8:14

A wise leader certainly arranges times for formal teaching, set aside for the dispensing of vital knowledge and instruction. However, the most effective teaching often happens when an alert leader takes advantage of one of those exceptional teachable moments that occur spontaneously.

In the incident cited above, the disciples obviously had not done what they should have done. They should have had a sufficient supply of bread for the trip across the Sea of Galilee. Jesus could have used this failure to teach them a lesson about supplies, logistics, checklists, and organization. He could have lectured them about the importance of paying attention to details. He could have said, "Just because my

Father made possible the feeding of four thousand with seven loaves, don't think this relieves you of the responsibility to plan for our own needs."

This *is* a lesson that some followers of some leaders need to be taught. Some followers develop such confidence in particularly effective leaders that they become careless in their own duties, thinking that the brilliance of the leader will always bail them out. However, Jesus chose to teach a much more fundamental lesson. From His example, we should learn to use those precious teachable moments to accomplish the greatest good.

At this moment in His ministry, Jesus faced the reality of an ever-growing opposition from the religious leaders of Israel. Their malignant hostility posed a greater threat to His mission than any lesser problems regarding logistics or scheduling. Seizing the moment, Jesus ignored those important areas in order to instruct His disciples about something that was both *important* and *crucial* to their future success. In doing so, Jesus took a teachable moment and turned it into an unforgettable floating seminar.

CHAPTER 18

BEWARE OF RISING YEAST

"Be careful," Jesus warned them. "Watch out for the yeast of the

Pharisees and that of Herod."

Mark 8:15

To know and understand your enemy is an important admonition. Good leaders understand the factors that will mitigate against the success of their enterprise.

There is one school of leadership that says, "Forget the competition. All we need to do is to focus on what we are doing, and we will be okay. Don't get distracted by what others are doing." This sounds good and *is* good, but only up to a point. You certainly don't want to become so mesmerized by what your adversaries are doing and get so caught up in countering them that you fail to execute as well as you possibly can. However, Jesus teaches us, as He taught His disciples here, that knowing your enemy will help you to overcome.

The best professional teams work endlessly on perfecting their own execution. At the same time, there are scouting operations which seek to know as much as possible about how their opponents play the game. The execution is then honed to be the best possible counter to their opponent's style of play. You don't neglect preparing to do your best, but you also learn how to best do it relative to your competition.

Our company is a relatively small one with only about 150 employees. On occasion we have found ourselves competing against some of the giants of international business. By careful observation we learned that their "pitch" would almost always center on their vast staff resources, on how many people they could bring to bear on a particular situation. By knowing about and understanding their tactic, we learned at least one way to try and counter it.

When faced with competing against a very large company, our approach to an athlete would be: "We can't promise huge numbers of people for your project, but what we can promise is that our very top people will be very personally involved. If you go with us, you won't be dealing with 'lieutenants.' You will have seasoned 'generals' taking daily personal responsibility for the success of the project." In other words, my partner and I would promise our own hands-on involvement. This often worked and we sometimes won against the giants. If we had not known about our competition, we could not have crafted a viable strategy.

Note another important point about Jesus' teaching. He draws the lesson by moving from the familiar to the unfamiliar. Seeing the disciples' one loaf of bread, He uses yeast to illustrate the evil intentions of Herod and the Pharisees.

This was a powerful illustration for two reasons. Every one of the disciples would have known all about yeast because it was so commonly used. Also, everyone understands that it only takes a little yeast to leaven an entire loaf of bread. It was the perfect illustration for the point Jesus wanted to make—a common substance known to all whose properties illustrated the pernicious nature of the evil working against them.

In telling them to "Watch out!" Jesus is teaching them that (1) there really are enemies out there, (2) the enemies are crafty and hard to spot, and (3) constant vigilance would be required to defend against them.

Wise leaders find simple ways to alert their followers to the dangers they face. In this case the disciples didn't at first grasp what He was saying. That only reinforces the importance of leaders' constantly teaching, teaching, teaching, and not assuming that their words are always immediately understood.

CHAPTER 19

MANAGING THE BIG PICTURE

"Be careful," Jesus warned them. "Watch out for the yeast of the

Pharisees and that of Herod."

Mark 8:15

Leadership, almost by definition, relates to the big picture. Successful leaders cannot get bogged down in minutiae. In most instances the details *must* be delegated. There are, however, some seemingly small things that, left unattended, will become big things and will prevent maximum good from occurring. In the verse above, Jesus was teaching about these kinds of things, the nonnegotiables.

A wise leader understands the difference between small, rather inconsequential details that do not merit time and attention, and those lapses which should set off loud sirens and start raising big red flags. There is a vast difference between forgetting to do something, even something important, and in being dishonest or in sowing disunity. The "yeast" Jesus was speaking about is evil. He was warning about the way it contaminates when it is introduced in even small amounts. This is a powerful lesson for those in leadership.

The "yeast" of Herod and the Pharisees was a growing corruption and evil disposition that, while small at this point, would eventually spread throughout the land. Jesus could clearly see the day coming when the small clouds on the horizon would eventually become thunderheads of controversy, breaking over His head amid the lightning and thunder of the last week of His life.

It's not as if the disciples were unaware of the opposition. They had experienced the hostility themselves; but like most followers, they couldn't see where it was leading. Jesus knew because He saw the future clearly. Here He moved to warn His men of the danger they themselves would face in the future.

Some problems a leader should overlook or, at most, quietly and privately mention about the needed correction to the person responsible. However, some kinds of problems should never be overlooked, and the entire organization should know that the leader has "hit the roof" over them. Dishonesty and disunity are two of these. At the very first sign of either, the leader should move swiftly and forcefully to deal with them. Never put these on the "back burner."

They, like other kinds of evil, will only grow and contaminate the entire operation.

By "hitting the roof," we do not mean that histrionics are in order and that a leader must yell and scream when faced with a situation which must be handled. We do mean that a swift and decisive action must be taken and that, somehow, the word must be delivered that dishonesty and disloyalty, even in small doses, will not be tolerated.

The kind of "buzz" you want to create is "Did you know that Marcia is no longer with us? I guess even petty cash is not considered petty around here." Or "The boss heard that Steve has been promising customers more than we could ever hope to deliver. Steve is not with us anymore." Or "You know Kevin, who is always spouting off about how bad our company is? Evidently he was told that if it was so bad, he should find somewhere else to work."

Leaders must be able to recognize the "yeast of the Pharisees" and be willing to deal with it immediately.

CHAPTER 20

A FOCUS ON FOCUS

"Do you have eyes but fail to see, and ears but fail to hear?

And don't you remember?"

Mark 8:18

Just as the disciples focused on the relatively minor problem of having no bread and, in their concern about it, demonstrated a lack of faith—particularly in the light of the great miracle they had just witnessed—followers today often become unfocused, forget past victories, and give in to fear and uncertainty. A leader must refocus, remind, and reassure.

In every kind of endeavor, from coaching a team to building a business to running a church, the leader must guard against a lack of focus. A leader must begin this vigilance with himself or herself. When a leader loses focus, the enterprise suffers. Too often, this lack of leadership focus leads to collapse and total failure.

When a corporate chief becomes enamored with a seemingly glamorous new undertaking that has nothing to do with the company's core business, problems ensue. When church leadership begins to see increased attendance (or some other secondary goal) as its primary goal instead of making obedient disciples, real blessings are sacrificed. Leadership must remain focused, must adhere to the mission statement. If a leader loses focus, all the others involved are sure to follow.

But how does a leader keep his own focus? The first few minutes of any day are very crucial for everything that follows. Does he or she spend time dedicating the day to God and asking for His direction? What about thinking strategically about the three or four most important things you need to do that day?

Some leaders have a mission statement they paste on their dashboard or on the mirror in the bathroom at home so it will never be far from their minds. I know other leaders who have a list of questions they ask themselves every morning:

1. What things do I need to do today that no one but I can do effectively?
2. What things on my list could be better done by someone else?
3. What problems have I been putting off because I don't want to deal with them?

4. What steps—however small—could I take today that will lead my company into the future?
5. What should I do today that will make me glad when today becomes yesterday?
6. How can I encourage the people around me today in what they have to do?

Questions such as these are vital because they force the leader to think about his priorities and help him stay focused. If he loses his focus, the people around him will soon lose theirs.

Note also the strategy Jesus followed to reassure His disciples:

1. He asked six very pointed questions.
2. The questions move from the problem to the root cause (unbelief caused by a bad memory).
3. He reminded them of two amazing miracles in the recent past.
4. He challenged them with the thought that by now they should have understood all of this without any explanation.

To call this reassurance may sound strange because it seems more like rebuke, but in reality Jesus was reassuring His disciples that despite their slow learning curve, He was still willing to work with them. He was also showing them that He had greater faith in them (and higher expectations) than they had for themselves.

No doubt it was no fun to be rebuked by Jesus; but in the end, the experience did them a world of good. It's like a highly respected coach telling his team, "You can do better, and because you can do better, I'm not going to be satisfied until that's exactly what happens." It stings, but the long-term impact produces followers who eventually become leaders.

CHAPTER 21

CALCULATE YOUR ACTIONS

MARK 8:22–26

He took the blind man by the hand and led him outside the village.

Mark 8:23

It is interesting to note that Jesus sometimes did things in unexpected ways. Obviously, He could have healed the blind man on the spot, right where he stood, without so much as lifting His finger. That He did not do so provides us with a valuable leadership lesson. It is important for leaders to understand that it is not only immediate results which count, but also the long-range impact the results will have. Sometimes it will be necessary to accomplish something "outside the villages" to achieve maximum positive impact. Too, the easiest way to get something done may not always be the best way to get it done.

This is the only place in the Gospels where Jesus healed in stages. Understanding why is made more difficult because the text doesn't clearly explain itself. Some obvious applications are:

1. Jesus does indeed have the power to open blinded eyes.
2. He has the power to heal instantly or in stages.
3. Jesus involved Himself in a very personal way in this man's problems.
4. He solved the problem in a way that also taught a lesson to His disciples.

Most commentators think that Jesus was teaching His disciples that they were like the blind man who had been partially healed. They saw Jesus dimly—not clearly—and they needed greater illumination from the Holy Spirit in order for their spiritual vision to clear.

Leaders of today, too, shouldn't be shocked that their followers are slow to grab the big picture. They must repeatedly and intentionally find moments when they can "teach by example" the overall mission of the organization.

It's worth noting that Jesus is here responding to a need of the moment. The man's friends brought him to Jesus. Healing a blind man wasn't on the day's agenda—speaking from a purely human point of view—but Jesus understood that this "interruption" actually provided a powerful moment for demonstrating His power, His compassion, and His commitment to His overall mission. He was "on task" even though the incident might have seemed like a distraction.

Incidentally, note that Jesus instructed the man not to go back into town. This, of course, would be the first place he wanted to go. This suggests that the miracle was being done not so much for public consumption but for the benefit of the disciples.

Wise leaders, like Jesus, will calculate their actions to produce the greatest good and to teach the most powerful lessons.

CHAPTER 22

ON THE ROAD AGAIN

Jesus and his disciples went on to the villages around Caesarea Philippi.

On the way he asked them, "Who do people say I am?"

Mark 8:27

This passage is full of lessons leaders need to learn. Perhaps the first is that a leader must be willing to go where the action is, must be willing to take the tough road trip. Jesus was headquartered in Capernaum, but we most often encounter Him on the road. And Caesarea Philippi was a particularly pagan city, a Greek city of some note in the first century.

Caesarea Philippi originally was a Canaanite center of Baal worship. Later it was named after the Greek god Pan. Still later Herod built a temple there in honor of Caesar Augustus. Finally Herod Phillip (a different Herod) expanded the city and renamed it after himself and the emperor Tiberius Caesar. Thus there was a strong Roman-Greek flavor to the town and an even stronger commitment to pagan worship. In spirit it was far removed from the cities and towns of Israel. Here Jesus was truly on "foreign soil."

Jesus did not just send His disciples into this tough area to pass out brochures; He led them into it. A quality leader often leads his troops into battle, he doesn't always just send them. As you lead, be alert for those occasions when the cause is best served by your presence. One corporate leader I know has a sort of rule of thumb which says, "The trip I want least to take is probably the one I should be certain to make."

A wise leader takes the tough trip with followers. On almost all occasions, Jesus traveled with His disciples and used the travel time to teach.

As we worked to build our company over three decades, some of the most profitable and rewarding times were spent traveling with our younger colleagues. I credit my partner with the wisdom of suggesting that even when the two of us were on the same plane, we should spend some of the flying hours with one of our younger associates. Those people are now in key positions. Jesus demonstrated this leadership lesson over and over.

CHAPTER 23

THE DISCIPLES' FINAL EXAM
———————— MARK 8:27–30 ————————

"But what about you?" he asked. "Who do you say I am?"

Mark 8:29

The film *The Bridge on the River Kwai* was one of the most compelling of all World War II motion pictures. In very dramatic fashion it tells a story which illustrates how easy it is for even the most intelligent and dedicated to become so focused on a secondary objective that the primary overarching goal is forgotten. In the film, the ranking British officer in a group of soldiers captured by the Japanese becomes so intent on using the building of a bridge as a way to maintain discipline and esprit de corps among his men that he forgets the reason they are there in the first place: to defeat the Japanese. A completed bridge will be a huge asset to the Japanese war effort. But because he has lost sight of the extremely important primary mission, he goes to even heroic efforts to build the bridge, thereby aiding the enemy.

A continuing theme of John MacArthur, noted pastor and Bible teacher, is how easy it is for the church to become distracted and to lose sight of its mission. Loss of focus causes even once-great churches to become insignificant. When this happens, so-called outreach committees focus on such trivia as ushers! No thought is given to the unchurched of the community except to work on how they would be directed to their seats should they happen to wander into the sanctuary! After creating order and insisting on unity, maintaining focus is the order of the day, every day, for leaders.

When Jesus asked the question in the key verse, He knew that before long He would hang on a cross. But before He could do that, He had to know where His men stood. He had to bring them out in the open. Were they with Him? Did they know who He really was? If you want to think of it in school terms, this was the disciples' final exam.

This time Jesus received a marvelous, thrilling answer from Peter. Often before, the answers to similar questions had told Him He had more teaching to do.

Jesus was one of the earliest proponents of public opinion research. In His question, He was gauging the impact of His message and His mission. It is very important for a leader not to lose touch with the people most affected by his or her leadership. To do this, a leader must have a close core of followers who have the confidence to tell him or her the truth.

Some leaders, early on, signal that they will tolerate only good news. This is a terrible mistake. The most valuable follower a leader can have is one who will deliver the tough truth. When a leader asks, "How am I doing?" (and this is a question that should be asked periodically), a trusted and trusting follower should be able and willing to give a truthful, unvarnished answer.

Be sure you engender this kind of trust in a group of close associates who will be willing to give you both the good news and the bad news, both about how you are doing and about how people perceive your leadership effectiveness. Use their truthful, honest answers to make your future leadership more effective.

CHAPTER 24

TRUE CONFESSION

"But what about you?" he asked. "Who do you say I am?"

Peter answered, "You are the Christ."

Mark 8:29

"Who do you say I am?" In the Greek text, that word *you* has an enormous stress. In fact, the *you* really goes at the first of the sentence. It is as if Jesus is saying, "But you who have followed Me and have known Me from the beginning, who do *you* say I am?" *It is the greatest question in all the universe, and it is one which every person must eventually answer.*

Peter answers for all the disciples. That's because he was the D. L.—the Designated Loudmouth. Whenever there was a question, Peter would always be the first one to answer. And when Peter answers here, he is not speaking simply for himself, but for all the disciples.

His answer is very, very specific: "You are the Christ."
Peter was saying, "I know who You are. You are the Messiah
sent to save us, and You are the Son of God from heaven." It
is short and simple. Everything necessary for salvation is
included in that statement.

Note that Peter said, "You are the Christ." Not "I say You
are the Christ" or "People say You are the Christ" or even
"We got together and took a vote and we think You are the
Christ." It is a declarative statement—"You are the Christ."

Some people would read that statement and say, "Well,
that's no big deal. I would say that, too." Most Christians
would probably stand up and say, "You are the Christ." But
Peter was the first person in human history ever to say it out
loud. And he said it when few were with Jesus and many
were against Him. He deserves all the credit, for without his
confession there would be no Christian church. In that sense,
there is a direct line between Caesarea Philippi and the Christian movement at the end of the twentieth century. We would
not be here if Peter had not opened his mouth.

A leader must earn the kind of affirmation Peter gave to
Jesus. Earning it, not expecting it or demanding it, should be
every leader's goal.

Leadership can be charted, analyzed, managed, ordered,
and, to some extent, manufactured. But in its most powerful
and important manifestation, it must be personal, emotive,
and, to some extent, spontaneous. The carefully drawn organizational charts only have life and real meaning to the extent

that, at key points, followers are saying to leaders, "I *will* follow *you*."

When this response comes, it is electrifying, energizing, and unifying. Leader and follower come together in a binding way, sealed together in a commitment to accomplish a worthwhile objective. This kind of bond is the most rewarding part of leadership and helps to make all the heavy costs of leadership worthwhile.

A leader earns the right to this special kind of relationship through an active involvement with his or her people. It is earned when care and concern are demonstrated. It is earned by accepting at least some of the same rigors followers are expected to undergo.

Be the kind of leader who earns the kind of affirmation that produces results.

CHAPTER 25

HOW TO DISPENSE NEWS
MARK 8:27–30

Jesus warned them not to tell anyone about him.

Mark 8:30

Obviously, Jesus wanted everyone to know who He was. He came to earth and invaded space and time "that they might know." He left behind all the glory that was His as a member of the Godhead so that men and women would come to *know* Him. He would suffer death, "even death on a cross," for the very reason that people should know Him and why He came. With all this in mind, the verse above becomes a tremendously powerful leadership lesson. When it is coupled with all the other instances cited in Mark and the other Gospels in which Jesus instructed both His disciples and others *not* to tell, we have a lesson for leaders not to be missed.

What seems to be an obvious non sequitur—Jesus' desire that all should know Him, and His many instructions not to tell, makes sense only when we understand that the timing, location, and method of releasing information determines its ultimate impact. The wisest leaders understand that information, like authority, is one of the basic tools of leadership. By virtue of position, a leader will have access to information that no one else will have. How and when that information is used will play a major role in determining the effectiveness of leaders.

Why did Jesus repeatedly tell His followers not to tell anyone else about Him? It boils down to two realities. First, His followers weren't ready for the news to be released. Even His inner circle still didn't have a full understanding of why He had come. Consider that just moments after Peter's amazing declaration of faith, Jesus rebuked him and said, "Get behind me, Satan!" Essentially, Peter clearly understood *who* Jesus was, but still didn't fully grasp *why* He had come.

In fact, the disciples would be in the dark regarding the crucifixion right up to the last moments of Jesus' life. They never really understood that Jesus *had* to die until after it happened. Jesus couldn't risk having the message go out publicly until His own key men fully grasped both His true identity and the mission God had given Him.

Second, the people of Israel weren't expecting a suffering Messiah. They were looking for a political/spiritual leader who could free them from Roman rule. If too many reports of His miracles were spread abroad, it might ignite a political movement that would divert Jesus from His mission as Savior of the world.

Did Jesus "manage" the news regarding who He was and why He came? Absolutely. To do otherwise was to risk ruining everything He came to do. At this critical point in His ministry, neither His key leaders nor the public at large were ready for the "good news" to be announced. That time would come. Jesus knew it, and He steadily moved toward that day. Until that day came, He steadfastly refused unnecessary publicity.

It is important to say here that in managing information, truth is never compromised or manipulated. Jesus never lied, never distorted the truth. Good leadership *always* is truthful leadership. It is how and when truth is used which is the subject of this lesson.

"Need to know" is one method leaders use to manage information. Important information is released primarily only to those persons and only at the time that they really *need* it, in order to advance the enterprise. A pastor and church leaders may be contemplating a very necessary move to new church facilities. To release that information to the total congregation before important decisions are made about the relocation would probably sow confusion and unnecessary concern. An effective leader will assess when that time has come.

In corporate life, a leader will often know well in advance when layoffs will be coming. How and when that information is released will determine how it impacts both the enterprise and individual lives. A wise and compassionate leader will balance those in the best way possible. He will make these kinds of decisions the subject of much prayer.

Jesus came to bring good news, the best of all possible news. The way He managed its "release" should be instructive to all leaders. Good news, good information, like bad, needs to be managed so that it will produce the greatest possible good. Jesus knew that necessary groundwork must be laid before the good news was declared for all to hear. He knew that timing was all-important. He had a plan that included when and how the news was to be made known to all. Effective leaders will never dispense information in a haphazard way.

One of the leadership lessons the life of Jesus teaches is that good news is most powerful when it is not dribbled out, but when it is released in a major way, at an important time to the right group of people. To manage news and information most effectively, it is important not to hold it too long. When leaks occur, even benign leaks, the news begins to manage you, as you must react and respond to it rather than the other way around.

Jesus used information very carefully. He managed it. Its use was an important and integral part of His plan. These are vital lessons for all leaders.

CHAPTER 26

PREPARING FOR THE HARD TIMES

He then began to teach them that the Son of Man must suffer many things

and be rejected by the elders, chief priests and teachers of the law, and

that he must be killed and after three days rise again.

Mark 8:31

Jesus began to prepare His disciples for the extremely difficult days ahead only after Peter's great affirmation, "You are the Christ." They had begun to grasp the good news about who Jesus was and why He came. Now they would need to understand the cost involved, the price to be paid, to be a part of Christ's mission. At this point, they had witnessed the healings, the miracles of feeding the masses, the casting out of demons, and even the control over weather. They had experienced the heady occasions when their Master had bounced around the haughty Pharisees by the power of His words. Now it was necessary for them to be prepared for the inevitable tough times.

Inevitable is a key word here. Wise leaders will understand that in every human endeavor of any scope or magnitude, there will be tough times. Difficulties *will* occur. The best leaders do all they can to prepare followers for these times of stress. Followers should never be taken by surprise by difficulties. As much as possible, surprises should always be on the "upside." Followers should not be able to say to a leader, "You never told us it would be like this."

As we examine the leadership of Jesus, we see that He very clearly and forcefully laid out the great promise of His mission: "I will make you fishers of men." Now it was necessary to lay out the great costs involved: "The Son of Man must suffer many things. . . ."

Consider the little word *must*. Behind it stands the full weight of all the prophecies of the Old Testament regarding the coming of our Lord. The word *must* reminds us that nothing that happened to Jesus happened by chance. All was predicted and foreordained by God's gracious plan. But this "must" leads on to suffering, pain, humiliation, and death. Can that be God's plan? Indeed it can and is—not just for Jesus, but for all of us.

There is much that might be said at this point regarding a proper theology of suffering. But this much is always true: God allows suffering to come to His children—to all of them sooner or later. Although salvation is free, the road to heaven is paved with "many dangers, toils, and snares."

Notice also that Jesus was very specific at this point. He would "suffer . . . be rejected . . . by the elders, chief priests and teachers of the law . . . he must be killed." The very specificity no doubt weighed heavily on the minds of the disciples. It's one thing to say, "I've got a bad feeling in the pit of my stomach." It's something else to say, "At 4 P.M. on Friday I'm going to be electrocuted." The fact that Jesus could state these things reveals something about His mastery of the circumstances and His confidence in His disciples. Even though they didn't fully grasp what He was saying, He "began" to unravel the dark side of the future.

Finally, Jesus also mentioned the resurrection—a fact the disciples grasped even less than His crucifixion. Since they really couldn't believe He would be killed, they seemed not to have understood the resurrection at all. But the bare mention of the resurrection was a way of giving ultimate hope to His followers: "Here's the light at the end of the tunnel." It's truly a dark tunnel, but what a light that shines from the empty tomb!

Followers should know about the risk/reward ratio. The greater the risk, the greater the reward. They should also know that risks cannot be avoided, so it is not foolish to take risks in a great and exciting cause. As Jim Elliot, the great missionary martyr, said, "He is no fool who gives what he cannot keep to gain what he cannot lose." Leaders of today need to be articulating both messages in cogent and powerful ways.

As leaders follow the example of Jesus, they will teach about and demonstrate the exciting possibilities of the effort to which they are committed. Followers and potential followers will get a realistic look at the upside, the rewards of success. This should motivate and excite them. However, a leader for the long haul will also, at the right time, clearly lay out the costs necessary to obtain that success: "For us to make it, all of us will have to put in a lot of hard work. There will be long hours and a great deal of travel involved. It will not be easy." Even the possibility of ultimate failure should be touched upon. "You know, no one has ever attempted this before. Even with our best efforts, we might not succeed" are statements to be considered.

I know all about the philosophy that says, "We will not even consider failure. We won't allow it to happen." That looks good as a slogan on a locker room wall, but it is not realistic in real life, in real human endeavors. No leader plans to fail, but many do. Almost all do at one point or another. The best and wisest prepare followers for this while leading and motivating toward success.

Jesus taught about both success and failure. He laid out the rewards to be obtained and the cost involved in obtaining them. He made sure there would be a minimum of unpleasant surprises. Great leadership!

CHAPTER 27

TOUGH LOVE

But when Jesus turned and looked at his disciples, he rebuked Peter.

"Get behind me, Satan!" he said. "You do not have in mind the things of

God, but the things of men."

Mark 8:33

In our "seeker-sensitive," politically correct world, where building a person's self-esteem is held to be a teacher's and a leader's highest goal, even the word *rebuke* seems archaic. Modern management and leadership theory would not support the kind of powerful, devastating rebuke Jesus gave Peter. This was no namby-pamby invitation to "sit down and talk this over" or to "see how we can reach consensus on this." It was no "I'm okay. You're okay" kind of transaction. This was a very pointed, forcefully delivered, scathing reprimand. The exclamation Mark included in the Scripture is there to show that this was a forceful pronouncement. And it was delivered in public. No one's feelings were spared with this one. A rebuke, even a stinging one, is a potent and valuable leadership device.

It is important to look at Jesus' rebuke of Peter in some detail. Perhaps the most important thing to note is its rarity. This kind of rebuke, far from representing a pattern of Jesus' leadership, was singular. This added to its great effect.

I know a corporate leader who is constantly, daily delivering rebukes of the magnitude and intensity of the one we are considering here. They have long since lost much of their positive impact. People get tired of them and begin to look for other jobs.

On the other hand, I played college basketball for a coach of the mildest manner. He almost never raised his voice. But on occasion, when our team had lost concentration and discipline, he really let us have it. His one rebuke was effective for an entire year! Those of us who were subjected to it still talk about it forty years later. The lesson is obvious: Use a strong rebuke rarely.

Secondly, it is important to be discerning about the person receiving the rebuke. Peter—bold, brash, and self-confident—could receive the rebuke and, while certainly stung, could rebound and come back stronger than ever from such a scolding. Jesus didn't deliver the rebuke to destroy Peter, but to build him up. However, this kind of rebuke might have destroyed John, a much more sensitive disciple.

Reserve your sharpest rebukes for your strongest followers. Use them to build up, not to tear down.

Too, use them where they will have a positive effect beyond the person to whom they are directed. The Scripture says, "But when Jesus turned and looked at his disciples, he rebuked Peter." He rebuked Peter, but the lesson was obviously for the entire group. You can be sure that all the disciples learned a great deal from the rebuke directed at Peter.

One of the most important and powerful lessons here is that, as a leader, Jesus demonstrated that none of His followers were beyond reproof and correction. Even Peter, who received Jesus' great affirmation, was still a follower subject to being taught by the leader. In all kinds of endeavors, those closest to the leader are sometimes those most in need of a rebuke, even a public one. They sometimes need "to be brought up short." When they are not, bad things happen, things that could have been prevented by a well-timed, well-placed rebuke.

A gifted and experienced elementary school teacher recalled the days when misbehaving students were routinely paddled—sometimes in front of the class, more often in the hallway. Why in the hallway? Because the sound of the paddling could be heard in many other classrooms. The teacher spoke of the hush that fell on the other students when he was giving some miscreant three whacks on the rear end. "I could paddle one boy and make three hundred others sit up straight," he said. Rebukes when done appropriately benefit many others besides the one being disciplined.

Why did Peter speak as he did to Jesus? Verse 32 says that Jesus was speaking "plainly" about His coming sufferings. Perhaps Peter felt He was being a bit too bold, too honest, too forthright. Maybe he thought that Jesus would only discourage the other men. He probably thought to himself, *I can handle this, but Thomas won't like it and Simon the Zealot will want to start a riot in Jerusalem. Better tell Jesus to lay off all this death talk for a while.* What's more, Peter handled the situation appropriately. He took Jesus aside and spoke to Him privately—which is exactly how a subordinate should speak to a leader in this situation.

That's what makes Jesus' rebuke so unexpected. I'm sure it blew Peter away. It seemed almost unfair and unkind. And it would be—unless truly important issues are at stake. If Peter had had his way, Jesus' mission would not have been accomplished; His whole purpose for coming to earth would have been foiled.

This shows how easily a key leader can—with good intentions—miss the larger picture and throw the whole organization off course. Jesus *had* to do what He did, hurt feelings or not, and not just for Peter's sake, but for all His men—who were probably thinking the same thing but were afraid to say it.

Finally, consider the phrase "Get behind me, Satan." It seems incredibly harsh—and even cruel. But Peter was really repeating (unwittingly) Satan's earlier attempt in the wilderness to distract Jesus from His mission of salvation. By calling Peter "Satan," Jesus indicated the source of Peter's wrong ideas and in a sense pointed the way toward forgiveness and restoration. "Peter, don't you see that I *must* die. If you oppose that, you are actually doing Satan's work. And if you want to follow Me, you must know that I will end up on the cross. There is no other way."

Suppose Jesus had said, "Get behind Me, Peter." That would have been a thousand times worse because it would be a personal rejection of the man—not simply of his misguided ideas. So there is grace hidden beneath this very stinging rebuke.

A strong public rebuke should never be given for anything but the most important of reasons. Jesus' rebuke of Peter was given only when the very core of His mission was threatened by Peter. A very pointed, very direct, not-to-be misunderstood rebuke was in order. Jesus delivered it.

Among the most important leadership lessons is that Jesus had "earned" the right to deliver a rebuke. Jesus had demonstrated His care for Peter from the time He gave him a personal call to follow, to the healing of his mother-in-law, to allowing him to witness many miracles, to singling him out for special teaching. Peter had to know that Jesus loved him and that even this kind of rebuke was delivered in love. Tough love, maybe, but love nevertheless.

As we lead, and as the need to rebuke presents itself, we need to be sure we have "earned" the right to deliver it. Our leadership should be of sufficient duration that both our commitment to the mission and our care for our followers have been clearly demonstrated. Only then should we consider the kind of rebuke Jesus gave Peter.

Even with all the conditions, considerations, and caveats, leaders should never forget the importance of a rebuke. It might not be a politically correct leadership technique, but it is an effective one. Jesus demonstrated this, and He is the greatest leader of all time.

CHAPTER 28

SPEAKING TO INSPIRE

Then he called the crowd to him along with his disciples and said:

"If anyone would come after me, he must deny himself and take up his

cross and follow me."

Mark 8:34

Too many leaders neglect the art of inspiring, challenging public speaking. This is a mistake because public speaking is a skill that everyone can develop. Practice, work, and determination can make any leader a better speaker and, thereby, a more effective leader.

Jesus used public speaking as one of His primary leadership tools. He spoke to instruct—as in the Sermon on the Mount and when He called the crowd to Him to teach about clean and unclean things—and to inspire and challenge—as in the passage cited here. He was a masterful public speaker. Leaders down through the ages have profited from His example. Abraham Lincoln, perhaps the most effective of American political speakers, is said to have modeled his speaking on the discourses of Jesus. Leaders today should do the same.

Note that Jesus' stinging rebuke of Peter, while done in the presence of the disciples, was *not* done before the general public—who wouldn't have understood it anyway. Also, Jesus' timing is obviously critical. He first secures an understanding from His key men regarding who He is. Only then does He lay out the suffering that is to come. And only after that does He rebuke Peter. Those were all "inside" tasks that had to be completed first.

Note the method Jesus used to gather the crowd's attention. He begins with the fact of His own popularity with the masses: "If anyone would come after me." That only makes sense if people were already attracted to His cause. But what will He ask for? Self-denial and the way of death.

"Take up your cross" has become a kind of proverb in Christian circles, so much so that we forget how radical it must have sounded in the first century. The cross was an instrument of Roman torture. At times the roads around Jerusalem were lined with hundreds of crosses bearing dead and dying men, their bodies bloated in the sun, surrounded by flies, covered with maggots. It's not a pretty thought or one calculated to win the masses. Yet that's the image Jesus calls to mind.

In Jesus' day, condemned criminals were made to carry the crossbar to the place of their own execution. Here Jesus is calling men to come and die in His service. We forget the shock of His words. He was calling His followers to heroic effort in the face of certain opposition, suffering, pain, and death. Not everyone would be willing to pay the price. By putting the matter so boldly, Jesus is "making the first cut" up front.

Great speakers understand that people respond to a great challenge — even one involving huge personal sacrifice when (1) they believe in the person making the challenge, (2) they see the challenge itself as being worthwhile, and (3) the challenge isn't sugarcoated but is put in stark, unforgettable terms. Too many public speakers mumble and drone when they would be far more effective if they said less and said it in a simple, direct way.

One of the most effective ways to become a better public speaker is to have someone you trust critique your speeches. Be sure this is someone who is not a "yes man," but someone you can count on to give you honest feedback. Jesus didn't need a critique. He *knew* how effective He was. None of us can be as sure.

Be a challenging, inspiring public speaker. It is a skill worth developing. Model your presentations after those of Jesus.

CHAPTER 29

CULTIVATING LOYALTY

"If anyone is ashamed of me and my words in this adulterous and sinful

generation, the Son of Man will be ashamed of him when he comes in his

Father's glory with the holy angels."

Mark 8:38

It's interesting to consider the background of this verse. From the disciples' point of view, there were many reasons to be ashamed of Jesus. First of all, He lacked the support of the religious/political establishment and was therefore an "outsider." Instead of leading a popular uprising, He set forth a spiritual kingdom that demanded things such as self-denial and taking up the cross—an abhorrent thought to first-century Jews. And Jesus Himself has just predicted His own suffering and eventual death—factors not likely to increase His public popularity. So these words are far from hyperbole.

As a good leader, Jesus knew that it would be easy for His men to give up and simply walk away. But note the promise implicit in His words: Those who stay with Me will share with Me when I gain the final victory at the end of time.

Finally, consider how personal this appeal is. If you are "ashamed" of Me, I will be "ashamed" of you. This speaks of the tight bond that exists between the best leaders and their followers. In the end, great leaders call forth such deeply personal loyalty that a man would rather die than cause his hero to be ashamed of him. This is the kind of challenge that caused the men at the Alamo to die for Texas and more than nine hundred Jews to commit suicide at Masada. Better to die for the cause than to live in shame.

Loyalty, like unity, with which it is closely allied, is a leadership absolute, an imperative. It is something that a leader should expect and on which he should be able to rely. Without loyalty, there really is no leader/follower relationship. A leader must cultivate and reward loyalty and must punish and expel those who are disloyal. This may seem harsh, but it is a leadership lesson of Jesus.

Loyalty does not mean mindless, uncritical devotion. That is worship, and no one other than Jesus is worthy of worship. Leaders make a grave mistake when they exercise the kind of leadership which requires any kind of submission. When this happens, leadership has degenerated into paranoia. This is not loyalty.

Loyalty is exercised primarily outside the group. Sometimes the most loyal thing a follower can do is to openly disagree with a leader. Because he cares about both the leader and the mission, he is willing to say, "Wait a minute. I think we are making a mistake here. Please explain to me why this is the best policy." These kinds of questions, openly asked of a leader, do not represent disloyalty. A wise leader should be open to answering honest questions and to dealing with honest disagreements. This builds and sustains both loyalty and unity.

Disloyalty occurs within the group when questions and disagreements are not openly asked and openly discussed. This sows disunity and must be curtailed. An even more serious kind of disloyalty occurs when followers do not support the leader and the mission outside the group, especially among the competition or opposition. This is the kind of thing Jesus was warning about in this passage. When a follower is disloyal and denigrates the leader or the endeavor outside the group, he is, in actuality, no longer a follower and should not be treated as such. Unless and until the disloyalty is dealt with and the person restored (as was the case with Peter later on), he should be expelled from the group.

A leader cannot and should not tolerate disloyalty. Jesus didn't.

CHAPTER 30

BOLD LEADERSHIP

MARK 9:1

And he said to them, "I tell you the truth, some who are standing here will

not taste death before they see the kingdom of God come with power."

Mark 9:1

The specific event predicted here evidently is the transfiguration, which occurred six days later. Here is a case where Jesus knew something His disciples would not have foreseen. They had no reason to expect that an event like the transfiguration was about to occur. Most likely they interpreted Jesus' comments to be a reference to the final setting up of the kingdom of God on the earth.

The timing is important. In the preceding verses we have Peter's confession, Peter's rebuke by Jesus, the challenge of cross-bearing, the call to total commitment, and the challenge of personal loyalty. The way is now cleared, so to speak, for the final portion of Jesus' public ministry. In racing terms, Jesus is now making the final turn into the homestretch. As He does so, He offers (via the transfiguration) a glimpse of His ultimate glory when He returns as King over all the earth. That vital experience will be increasingly important as the opposition grows and as the final days of Jesus' life are played out amid controversy, suffering, and death.

So we can say that Jesus, knowing what the future would hold, picks an opportune moment to make a bold statement—which His men wouldn't immediately understand—that leads to an experience which would prepare them emotionally for the hard times to come.

The most powerful and effective leadership is bold leadership. It is not rash. It does not promise what it cannot deliver. It does not go in for "grandstand plays," those showy performances which serve primarily to build personal ego. Just as Jesus used this occasion to make a bold and powerful assertion, wise leaders will look for occasions when they can make their own prudent, but potent and provocative statements.

Dave Dixon, the imaginative and innovative sports entrepreneur, made two of the boldest statements ever made in American sports. The first was that we were going to build the greatest sports stadium in the world. We did, the Superdome in New Orleans. The second was, in some ways, even bolder. I was visiting his home in New Orleans and, out of the blue, he turned to me and said, "Bob, you and I are going to take over tennis and turn it into a major spectator sport worldwide." Sure, Dave. Neither of us had ever even seen an official tennis match, but Dave Dixon was the kind of bold leader who turned bold statements into bold reality. In fact, we did take over tennis; and the $100 million-plus worldwide professional tennis circuit is the result of what we did. A bold leader makes calculated, bold statements which motivate and energize followers into making them come true.

As bold as He was, Jesus never promised more than He could and would deliver. In this, and in all things, He should be our pattern.

CHAPTER 31

WHY INTIMACY IS IMPORTANT

After six days Jesus took Peter, James and John with him and led them

up a high mountain, where they were all alone. There he was

transfigured before them.

Mark 9:2

Mark doesn't tell us why Jesus singled out James, Peter, and John to go with Him to the mountain. They definitely seem to have been part of His inner circle from the earliest days of His ministry. They were among His first followers, were present at some miracles the others did not witness, and were always mentioned first in every listing of the apostles. This suggests that Jesus established a close relationship with these three from the very beginning—a relationship the rest of the disciples acknowledged, even if they did not fully understand.

Note that Jesus apparently makes no explanation as to why these three men are chosen and others are not. Certainly He saw them as representative of the others and knew they would tell the others what they had experienced. By this point in Jesus' ministry, the other nine men knew that James, Peter, and John had an intimate relationship with the Lord; so no explanation was needed. In any case, no leader can ever fully explain why he is drawn to one person and not to another. In most cases, it's better not to try to explain it.

More leadership has failed from a lack of intimacy than from any other cause. Leaders, no matter how brilliant, cut their tenures short or accomplish less than they might otherwise when they fail to establish close relationships with a few key people, a core of their followers. I have been in situations where followers, including myself, sought a closer relationship with a leader, not for personal gain, but for his sake and for the sake of the enterprise—only to be rebuffed. Every time a leader tries to "go it alone," something less than the best occurs.

The very nature of leadership requires some distance between a leader and the bulk of his or her followers. It is impossible to lead and to be close with everyone. However, the very nature of leadership also requires a close, intimate relationship characterized by a degree of vulnerability with at least *some* followers. Too, the more demanding, complex, and stressful the undertaking, the more a closeness with an inner core becomes necessary. Certainly a church, a school, a team, and almost all business endeavors require that a leader develop an intimacy with a core group in order to *produce* maximum success for all concerned. To accept the cliché "It is lonely at the top" is to accept a leadership style which will deliver less than it should.

Pastors, even those in large churches, are among the leaders who find it most difficult to establish a close, honest, caring relationship with an inner core of believers. In some cases, the more gifted a pastor is in the preaching ministry, the more possibility there is that he will increasingly isolate himself from others. This is a recipe for difficulty and sometimes for tragedy. Of all leaders, pastors are most in need of the kind of fellowship, support, and honest criticism they can receive from a small inner circle. For a look at the positive side of this, I suggest *Unveiled Hope* by Scotty Smith and Michael Card, which details how the dynamic Christ Community Church in Franklin, Tennessee, was built on the ideal of intimacy and accountability.

Leaders who fear intimacy will look for all kinds of excuses to avoid it. One of the most common, particularly in the church, is: "I can't be seen showing favoritism by getting too close to any one group of people. I must treat everyone the same." This is not only nonsense; it is not scriptural.

The results of Jesus' investment in a particularly close relationship with Peter, James, and John are very evident. James was the first disciple put to death for his commitment to Jesus. John went on to write his Gospel, three letters, and the marvelous Book of Revelation. And of course Peter, along with Paul, became a most important leader of the church. All the disciples would eventually become leaders in the early church, but these three would be in the first rank. Jesus knew that and chose them to share in the intimate transfiguration experience with Him.

Leaders must develop a core group of followers in whom they confide and from whom they expect honest feedback and wholehearted support. Building this core may not be easy. There may be fits and starts. Some chosen for it may not themselves be ready for the kind of relationship it requires. There may be some pain involved. Regardless, it is well worth it. In fact, quality long-term leadership is not possible without it.

CHAPTER 32

THE POWER OF OUTSIDE AFFIRMATIONS

MARK 9:2–11

Then a cloud appeared and enveloped them, and a voice came from the

cloud: "This is my Son, whom I love. Listen to him!"

Mark 9:7

Jesus had a special reason for taking Peter, James, and John with Him to witness the transfiguration and to hear the voice from the cloud. Jesus was continually giving them a basis to believe the amazing things He was telling them. Particularly, He was preparing them for the excruciating times which were now looming close. It was a good thing He did. Even with all the miracles performed in their presence, even with all the brilliant teaching conducted in their hearing, and even with this awesome, transcendent experience of the transfiguration, their belief flickered and went out or, at least, burned very low at the time of the arrest and crucifixion.

Evidently the transfiguration made a huge impact on Peter, who mentioned this event some thirty years later near the end of his life. In 2 Peter 1:16–18 Peter recalls this momentous event and uses it to argue for the truth of the gospel. He *knows* the gospel is true because he heard the voice from heaven—a voice he could never forget. Therefore (he is arguing), his words can be trusted because he was there as an eyewitness on the mountain. He saw what happened; he heard God's voice. It's all as real to him as an old man as it was the day he first heard it.

This is *exactly* why Jesus took Peter up to the mountain in the first place. He wanted Peter to never forget that moment—and he never did. This is great leadership: a perfect sense of timing and the creation of an impression that would last long after the leader had left the scene.

Without self-aggrandizement or for ego's sake, a leader needs to build his stature among his followers. This needs to be done primarily by an obvious commitment to them and their shared mission. However, a wise leader will also look for opportunities to have outside sources confirm his worth to followers.

When a leader is asked to speak to an outside group, it is important to take along at least one or two followers so they can see the esteem in which their leader is held by those outside the group. Just as Peter, James, and John must have done, they will pass on what they have seen and heard to other followers. If a leader is given a significant honor, such as an industry award or an honorary doctorate, this is a great opportunity to have followers present and, if possible, to participate.

One of the most important reasons for a leader to submit to media interviews and to accept outside writing assignments is to enable followers to read or hear what is written or said. A most important audience is the one inside the organization. "Hey, did you see what the *Times* said about the boss?" or "Did you catch the chief on TV last night?" are the kinds of comments that help to cement a leader's place among his or her followers.

As with everything, balance and discernment is necessary. A leader does not want to be seen as a "publicity hound." But in thoughtful, measured ways, and with the goal of strengthening leadership and advancing the cause, outside affirming exposure is valuable.

Obviously, Jesus was the furthest thing possible from an egomaniac. Yet He made sure He did not go through the transfiguration experience alone. He did not want it "wasted" as a teaching experience for His followers. This is an important lesson for every leader to learn.

CHAPTER 33

LINGERING ON THE
MOUNTAINTOP

MARK 9:2–12

Peter said to Jesus, "Rabbi, it is good for us to be here. Let us put up

three shelters—one for you, one for Moses and one for Elijah."

Mark 9:5

Like Peter, wouldn't we all rather stay up on the mountain and enjoy the presence of the Lord? In Peter's defense, who wouldn't want to stay awhile when such amazing things are happening?

Think about the setting. They are up on the mountain when suddenly Peter sees Jesus radically and wonderfully transfigured. Then suddenly out of nowhere, Moses and Elijah show up. Hey, what are those two guys doing here? Evidently their presence serves to confirm that Jesus is indeed the promised Old Testament Messiah. They didn't appear for Jesus' sake, but for the sake of James, Peter, and John.

Peter's response is understandable in light of what was happening. He literally didn't have a clue as to what it all meant, but his first statement is certainly true—"It is good for us to be here." Most commentators suggest that Peter's idea of the shelters was an unspoken attempt to enjoy the glory of Christ without the sufferings that must precede it. We might say that his impulse was understandable but clearly wrong because Jesus had already told them that His suffering must precede His coming in glory.

There is always a time to work, and then there is a time to enjoy the fruits of your labor. First the cross, then the resurrection, is always God's pattern. That order can never be reversed. Peter had a very hard time accepting the reality that his Master would have to die, so he found every possible reason to avoid that awful moment. It was a misguided sense of love and loyalty that caused him to do these things, which is why Jesus even in His severe rebukes never rejects Peter but constantly points him back to the mission. This means enjoying the mountain while you are there, but understanding that eventually you must go back into the valley where the cross awaits.

Success and prosperity affect different people in different ways. For some, success only whets the appetite and is energizing. For others, success produces self-satisfaction and a debilitating complacency. Real leaders, particularly those in the church, are not there to manage the status quo but to lead to new heights and new victories.

Unfortunately, it is in the church where this seems to be the most difficult. In no other segment of society is complacency a bigger problem. Across the church in America the most intense current discussions are about worship styles! They should be about reaching the lost, being "salt," or making disciples. This is the current version of "Let us put up three shelters. . . ." Vigorous, robust leaders, the kind Jesus models for us, never give in to this kind of complacency, but either jump-start the situation and get it moving or move on themselves. While watching for complacency in followers, leaders must also watch carefully for it in themselves.

As Jesus led the disciples down from the mountain, He taught them and further equipped them for the job ahead. The awesome magnificence of the transfiguration provided the ultimate teachable moment. Jesus took full advantage of it. He made sure the three knew that this was the time to move. He, Jesus, was there; and He was all they needed to get on with the task at hand.

This is real leadership. Today's leaders, particularly those in the church, need to help followers understand that *today* is the day of salvation. Not only has John the Baptist already come; Jesus has already come and accomplished His mighty work, and the Holy Spirit has already come, bringing power and direction. This is no time to build three shelters and sit down. This is a time to move in faith, with vigor and determination.

CHAPTER 34

CONTROL THE FLOW OF INFORMATION

As they were coming down the mountain, Jesus gave them orders not to

tell anyone what they had seen until the Son of Man had risen from the

dead. They kept the matter to themselves, discussing what

"rising from the dead" meant.

Mark 9:9–10

The disciples couldn't figure out what "rising from the dead" meant. To us it seems simple, but that's because we live on this side of the empty tomb. And we accept it by faith. None of us have ever physically seen a person rise from the dead. The disciples were clueless, perhaps wondering if Jesus was referring to some general resurrection from the dead at the end of history or if the phrase meant some kind of "spiritual resurrection." At this point they simply had no way to grasp

Jesus' personal death and His physical, bodily resurrection—even though He had clearly predicted both events.

Some things simply can't be understood until they are put in proper context. The transfiguration, at the time, seemed like an amazing event. It didn't "fit" until after Jesus rose from the dead. Then and only then did the disciples understand it as a prefiguring of Jesus' ultimate return to the earth in power and great glory.

Jesus knew that the three disciples could not yet understand the transfiguration and its significance. They certainly could not properly convey its meaning to the others at this time. In this passage, we again see Jesus "managing" the news and information flow. Obviously, He had a complete and perfect understanding of timing and how best to use the facts at hand. Today's leaders need to follow His example to the fullest extent possible.

Jesus provides an ideal pattern for leaders to follow. To release information not fully understood, with its implications unclear, is to create doubt and confusion instead of confidence and orderly progress. A wise leader needs to understand how valuable, even precious, information is. It needs to be seen as a perishable resource, to be used at "its peak of freshness," but not before it is "ripe."

This concept is understood so well in financial circles that there are very strict laws governing the release of information. In the past decade, several high-profile financiers have spent time in jail for misusing information and manipulating the timing of its release for their own benefit and to the detriment of others. Corporations with major announcements to make wait for the stock markets to close before making them, allowing time for everyone to receive the information and react to it in an orderly way.

Of course, Jesus used information and the news He created in ways that would advance His cause—the most noble cause ever conceived. With Jesus as their example, wise leaders will continually work to refine their communication skills.

CHAPTER 35

THE FREEDOM TO FAIL

MARK 9:14–29

"Whenever it seizes him, it throws him to the ground. He foams at the mouth, gnashes his teeth and becomes rigid. I asked your disciples to drive out the spirit, but they could not."

Mark 9:18

Good leaders recognize the importance of giving their followers a chance to fail sometimes, knowing that failure is generally a much better teacher than success. After all, if the disciples had worked this miracle on their own, it might have puffed them up with pride. By allowing them to fail—and in a very public way at that—Jesus humbled them and made them very willing to listen to what He had to say.

Note also that this "failure" comes on the heels of the transfiguration. It's a reminder that "mountaintop experiences" are no substitute for simple faith in God, as expressed in believing prayer. Perhaps "the boys" felt a little cocky after Peter, James, and John shared what they had seen and heard. If so, this humiliating failure would quickly bring them back to reality.

Sometimes leaders must give their people chances to succeed or fail on their own—and then be ready to help them no matter what happens. And sometimes we must let our people fall on their face in front of many people, which, by implication, will probably embarrass us as well.

Keep the goal in view. You want leaders who can reproduce themselves in others, which means having the confidence to take decisive action even at the risk of occasional failure.

CHAPTER 36

CALL FORTH FAITH

"If you can?" said Jesus. "Everything is possible for him who believes."

Mark 9:23

Over and over Jesus demonstrates the power of words—the right words for the right occasion. He constantly shows us that leadership is much more than titles, charts, and directives. Leadership, to accomplish its highest purposes, must be based on inspired and inspiring communication.

It is easy to say that telling someone to be an inspirational leader is like telling someone to be taller. This is the easy way out, the fatalistic view. True, some people have more innate flair than others, but we can all add to the amount we have.

We need to work on inspiration to be inspired. We need to be conscious of the need to add inspirational communication to our repertoire of leadership skills. We need to "go to school on" inspirational leaders of the past. This is what we are doing with this book. We are studying the most inspirational leader of all time—Jesus.

One of the things Jesus teaches us about inspirational communication is that for us to be effective with it, we must be there. This may seem so obvious as to sound ridiculous. However, many of today's leaders fail to show up at opportune times, when inspirational communication could be delivered.

How often do we read or hear that "A spokesperson for XYZ had the following statement to make. . . ." I find myself asking, "Where's the top guy? I want to know what he says and how he says it." Leaders often miss making the impact they could by failing to put in a personal appearance in crucial situations. Hiding behind a "spokesperson" is easy, but not productive.

I think many leaders choose not to make a personal appearance because they haven't practiced and prepared for occasions when the enterprise can best be served by their presence. Obviously, Jesus was very well prepared. In an earthly sense, He had studied the Scriptures, the basis for almost all His public remarks. He had "showed up," even as a boy, to exchange views with the leaders of His day.

It is certainly true that a leader needs to be selective about showing up personally. Jesus demonstrated this brilliantly by using John the Baptist to pave the way for Him. The key here is the phrase "pave the way." A spokesperson is most useful as one who "sets up" the leader for an important communication. If John the Baptist had had the last word instead of preparing the way for Jesus to have the last word, the plan and the communication would have been incomplete.

In the passage we are considering, Jesus used the pithy phrase "If you can?" as a means of awakening the father's dormant faith. Sometimes leaders recognize potential in others that they themselves do not see or feel. The issue isn't the father's desire for his son to be made well—that much is abundantly clear by his bringing the son to the disciples in the first place. But will he now place his faith in Jesus alone, or will the disciples' failure so utterly discourage him that he won't believe anything at all?

I find the father's reply honest—and heartening. How often do we all say, "I believe—help my unbelief." All true faith is mixture of belief and unbelief. Yet that little belief was more than enough for Jesus to perform a mighty miracle of healing.

Once again we see the world's greatest leader calling forth faith from a man who didn't know he had it in him. All it took was a little phrase—a simple question—a "word fitly spoken" by the Master.

You don't have to say a great deal. Sometimes just a few words at the right moment can work wonders.

CHAPTER 37

ONLY BY PRAYER

He replied, "This kind can come out only by prayer."

Mark 9:29

To consider the leadership lessons of Jesus and not to include the importance of prayer would be unthinkable. Prayer was a major part of His life and teaching. Not to fully appreciate this is to have an incomplete and distorted picture of how Jesus lived and how He led.

He used prayer in several ways. All should be instructive to us. First of all, He was a man of prayer. He prayed both in private and in public. He used prayer to order His day. Earlier in Mark, we find that Jesus got up very early in the morning, "while it was yet dark," to pray. It was a part of the discipline of His life. Leaders in today's hectic world can use prayer as a way to structure and focus the day. This is not in any way to say that prayer is not powerful, important, and necessary in and of itself. It is. But two key ways to use prayer are to begin a day and to bring closure to a busy day.

Secondly, Jesus was *an example* of a man of prayer. His disciples, those He led, had to have been struck by this. They saw what a major part prayer played in His life, adding to the confidence they felt in following Him.

Even in today's cynical world, we believe that followers in every area of life will have a higher level of confidence in a leader who includes prayer in his or her life. Certainly, there will be those who sneer. Lose an important account and someone will be sure to say, "Well, the old man's prayers didn't help us on that one." Fail to reach a fund-raising goal, and the equivalent of "Maybe we should have worked harder and prayed less" will probably make the rounds. All this notwithstanding, most people would rather follow a leader who is a man or woman of prayer.

Jesus also taught about prayer. The Lord's Prayer is the best example of this. To some it may seem sort of fey and otherworldly to teach about prayer in today's situations. Of course, prayer *is* otherworldly. That is one of the most important reasons to recommend it.

More and more people in every walk of life are looking for the transcendent. All the New Age hype and interest in pseudo-spiritual things is evidence of this. A leader who teaches the basics of true prayer to the true God cannot go wrong.

In the key verse, Jesus demonstrated the absolute necessity of prayer in some situations. There will be times when the most appropriate thing a leader can say is, "Without God's intervention, this won't happen." Some things can only be brought about by prayer. Jesus seemed to indicate that from time to time we will encounter a "this kind" of problem—some situation so overwhelming that it simply outstrips our resources. God brings us "this kind" of problem so that we will learn and relearn that our dependence must be on God alone.

Loneliness and isolation are major problems for people in business, particularly those who must travel and be apart from their families. Wise leaders will point their key people to prayer as a most effective way to combat this. It fell my lot to be one of the first Americans to go into the People's Republic of China after the end of the terrible "Cultural Revolution" in that country. I was going in, not as an American, but as the head of an international sports organization. (This was before there was a functioning American embassy there.) A condition of my entering the country was that I go alone; the Chinese were very wary of foreigners in those days.

The evening before I was to board a People's Republic government jet in Tokyo to fly to Beijing, Akio Morita, the legendary founder of Sony, graciously gave me one of Sony's most sophisticated shortwave radios to take in with me. He said, "Once you get in the Chinese jet, you will be completely cut off from any communication. You won't be able to reach anyone outside China. With the radio you will at least be able to hear from people outside China."

Mr. Morita was wrong. In the isolation of China, I was able to reach my heavenly Father more easily and directly than ever before. I had no phone or fax, but prayer more than sustained me during those strange days. I missed my family and friends, but prayer kept the loneliness at bay.

There is no substitute for prayer—especially when we face the impossible problems of life.

CHAPTER 38

THE INNER CIRCLE

They left that place and passed through Galilee. Jesus did not want

anyone to know where they were, because he was teaching his disciples.

Mark 9:30–31

Some leaders resent the time taken away from "real work" to teach and train those they lead. In our own company we have to battle the tendency to schedule "work" sessions even during our corporate retreats. We reason that we cannot afford to take time away from the basics of our business.

Leaders need to learn from Jesus. His example shows that teaching is not an interruption of the mission, but *it is the mission.* As leaders internalize this and make it the centerpiece of their leadership style, great progress is made. Wise, effective leaders make sure that teaching has the highest possible priority.

Much conventional wisdom would say that as Jesus moved through Galilee, He should have taken the opportunities to address the crowds He could easily attract. Make the pitch, sell the product, influence the masses, make the numbers count, take it to the streets—these are often seen as imperatives by many leaders.

We see Jesus taking the exact opposite approach. He turned aside from the multitude of potential "customers" in order to teach His small band. What a powerful, potent, pointed lesson for all leaders!

Because Jesus placed a higher priority on teaching His disciples than on communicating the message to the masses, untold millions around the world and down through the ages have been blessed. The marvelous things the disciples were able to do after Jesus left them were the result of His putting teaching them first on His agenda. The church that blesses the world today, and which will continue to do so until Jesus comes again, is the result of this strategy.

Jesus was actually *reteaching* what He had already taught them previously. The disciples had a hard time grasping how suffering and death (much less a resurrection) could fit into God's plan for Jesus. Several commentators note that all three synoptic Gospels emphasize that the closer Jesus came to His final week in Jerusalem, the more time He spent teaching His disciples in private. This of course would climax in the great upper room discourse (John 13–17) on the night before He died.

The disciples seemed to be afraid to ask Him about His coming death and resurrection. Perhaps they thought the whole subject too morbid. Maybe they couldn't figure out what questions to ask, or perhaps they feared being rebuked as Jesus had earlier rebuked Peter. At this point, it's instructive that Jesus is content to simply reiterate His earlier teaching. No doubt He knew of their confusion, but didn't try to "force the issue." Patient teaching, repeated over time, would eventually help them understand. But in the end, their faith would be severely tested—and even shattered—by His death. No amount of teaching could fully prepare them for what was to come.

Jesus at this point gives them as much as they are prepared to receive. Later He will teach them much more. But for the moment He leaves some questions deliberately unanswered. This is also good leadership strategy.

Mass communication and the constantly emerging technology which makes this more and more powerful should certainly be co-opted for today's enterprises. We must use these tools as effectively as possible. However, it is more important to remember that the most effective teaching is always based on this rule: "The smaller the number, the more powerful the communication."

Jesus preached to the masses, but He *taught* His disciples. He saved His most important teaching for only three of these: Peter, James, and John. When He wanted to be sure an important point was made, He went one-on-one with them.

Leaders need to be sure that while they are utilizing all the communication tools at their disposal, they are giving the highest possible priority to teaching those few closest to them. A leader needs to plan for those times when he does "not want anyone to know where they are" so he can teach. No phones, no faxes, no E-mail, no "work" agendas—just teaching.

The results of this kind of teaching priority will be long-range and far reaching. It is the way Jesus led.

CHAPTER 39

THE SERVANT LEADER

"If anyone wants to be first, he must be the very last, and the servant of all."

Mark 9:35b

After all Jesus has said and done—after all His miracles and the repeated teachings—what were these guys talking about on the road? They were arguing about who was the greatest. Unbelievable!

In the Jewish society of that day—as in most societies in every generation—there was a huge emphasis on power, position, prestige, and titles. "Who's number one?" is still the operative question. Because He knew their hearts, Jesus knew about their sinful ambition even before He asked what they were arguing about. Like little children caught misbehaving, they were ashamed to answer Him.

At that point He could have rebuked them again, but instead He chose this moment for an unforgettable teaching experience. He did it by giving another of His pithy sayings: "To be first, you must be last."

None of Jesus' leadership lessons may seem more paradoxical than the servant/leader concept, which is, in fact, the very essence of both His leadership example and His leadership teaching. The concept of the servant/leader is difficult for many to grasp at the end of the twentieth century, in part because today's leadership literature espouses just the opposite and glorifies a different kind of leader altogether. Literature extolling Atilla the Hun, telling us "you don't get what you deserve, you get what you negotiate," and generally teaching a me-first, in-your-face, slash-and-burn leadership style is the norm.

To think that a leader can succeed by putting his or her followers and customers first, both individually and as a group, seems wrongheaded, unworkable, and a formula for failure. In fact and in truth, this leadership lesson of Jesus is the single surest formula for success ever enunciated. It is a guarantee of success in the broadest, most lasting sense. Think about it. If you are leading a company and you put your employees, colleagues, and customers first, you are on the road to success. On the other hand, if the bottom line comes first, no matter what, you are likely headed for abuses and disaster.

The lessons of Jesus only *seem* to be paradoxical. They are, in fact, clear-eyed, ultimately workable, and eminently practical. Best of all, they work in time and for eternity.

Putting others first and becoming the servant of all does not mean going soft and namby-pamby. Jesus certainly never taught that or demonstrated that. He did not come to satisfy every whim or to meet everyone's perceived need. He did not condone or put up with position jockeying, personal aggrandizement, selfishness, or greed. Hypocrisy, arrogance, and pride generated His disdain. He was forceful and direct when confronting attitudes and actions that were in opposition to both His overall mission and His followers' ultimate long-range good.

Too, it is obvious that He looked for and expected continual improvement in the disciples' understanding and action. He taught to accomplish this. He led to obtain this result. Jesus shows us that he who serves best and teaches best *leads* best. Discipline, administered through thoughtful rebukes, was a part of His servant leadership.

Serving all, in the way Jesus teaches, is not only about washing feet; it is also about leading followers into commitment, into dedication, into discipline, and into excellence. Strangely, it is in the church where this kind of servant leadership is most rarely seen. Many pastors and church leaders seem to expect to *be* served, with the programs of the church revolving around showcasing them. On the other hand, there are almost no expectations for the rank and file of church members beyond the hope that they will show up and contribute funds. The word *discipline,* clearly called for in the New Testament, is almost never even whispered.

No one is putting others and the mission first in the way Jesus taught. The kind of leadership He calls for is costly in the kind of commitment it takes and in the kind of discomfort it produces. It is, however, true servant leadership. It does produce success.

In the kingdom of God, the way up is down. Jesus overturned contemporary notions of power and replaced them with the paradox of servant leadership. In a sense He was saying, "It doesn't matter who has the title. Look for the one with the servant's heart, and there you've found your leader." As in all other areas, He Himself is the perfect example.

CHAPTER 40

CHILDREN ARE WELCOME HERE
MARK 9:33–37

"Whoever welcomes one of these little children in my name welcomes me;

and whoever welcomes me does not welcome me but the one who sent me."

Mark 9:37

"We are a business, not a charity." This was the reaction of a corporate chairman, when looking at a board meeting agenda prepared by his assistant that had a line item reading "Children." The company did not sell products for children, but was primarily engaged in working with Fortune 500 companies and their marketing. The chairman could not see why he and the board should waste time talking about children. His attitude was wrongheaded and went against the leadership lessons of Jesus.

Both by His teaching and His example, Jesus underscored the importance of children. Again, it might seem paradoxical, with so much to do in so short a time period, that He would take so much time to talk about children, use children as a positive example, and spend precious time with them. A key to understanding this is to understand that children were not ancillary to His mission; they were an integral part of it. "Children" should be a line item on the agenda of every leader.

Regardless of the enterprise you are leading, your primary question should always be, "How does what we do affect children?" This should be a leadership question because it is right, because it follows Jesus' teaching and example, *and* because dealing with it will, in very practical and tangible ways, contribute to success.

Children are not primarily a charitable issue or a social issue. They are primarily a leadership or an enterprise issue. The more you consider children and their needs, the more successful your leadership will be. Too, you and those you lead will feel much better about both the enterprise and yourselves if you have dealt with the "children question."

First, consider the children of those involved in your undertaking. Ask, How will our schedules, what we ask of the people involved, impact the lives of our children? Also ask, How can we be a positive influence on children at large? These are questions for every enterprise. Leaders take note. I hope it is needless to say here that we should never, never exploit children. Both the public at large and law enforcement agencies come down particularly hard on those who use children for ill-gotten gain. Just ask those hapless executives who allowed their company to try to pass off colored water as juice for children.

Unfortunately, in many churches children and their needs are the last to be considered. Choice people to minister to them, their programs, their classrooms, and their supplies are considered last. They should be first. The so-called "seeker-friendly" churches have proven that if a priority is given to great programs for children, the adults will flock to that place. Churches whose programs are so demanding on adult members that their children are neglected do not succeed. They go against a principal leadership lesson of Jesus.

Tragically, leaders of churches and schools today must be cognizant of the threat that children can be abused while in their care. Without becoming paranoid, leaders must be very prudent in safeguarding children against deviants who might target churches and schools as places to gain access to them.

We sometimes sing "Jesus loves the little children." How do we know that? Because He took a tiny infant in His arms and used him to teach important spiritual truth.

As a leadership principle, this is one of our Lord's most powerful object lessons—one that still stirs the heart two thousand years later. In almost every church nursery there is a picture of Jesus holding a baby, surrounded by His disciples. It is an image that has helped to create hospitals, orphanages, infant welfare societies, Sunday schools, and children's missionary agencies around the world.

Jesus loved the little children, and so should we.

CHAPTER 41

THE "NOT INVENTED HERE" SYNDROME
———————— MARK 9:38–41 ————————

"Teacher," said John, "we saw a man driving out demons in your name

and we told him to stop, because he was not one of us."

Mark 9:38

The "not invented here" reaction to good ideas is a problem
with which all leaders must deal. In selling television advertising, we came to believe we had to convince most advertising agencies that what we were proposing was really their
idea in the first place, if we were to have any possibility of
making a deal.

Many very good ideas are lost, or end up benefiting someone else, because of the "not invented here" prejudice. Some
people have an attitude which says, *If we didn't think of it, it
must not be any good.* Leaders must fight this and convince
followers to accept and co-opt good ideas from all sources,

giving credit where credit is due. A way for a leader to engender this very productive practice is to recognize and reward people who are committed enough to discern a good idea and to champion it even though it originated with someone else.

Competition in and of itself isn't wrong or evil. But when all you do is count "nickels and noses" or when your only measure of success is the bottom line, you risk measuring everything you do by the standards of the world.

This passage reminds us that God's work is far bigger than our limited vision. God has His people in many places—often doing things that we ourselves could never do. When the disciples come complaining about this man who worked miracles but not under their jurisdiction, Jesus basically says, "Leave him alone." He doesn't say, "Make an alliance with him" or "Invite him to join us." It's simpler than that. "Just leave him alone. Let him serve Me in his own way."

By implication, the message is, "You take care of your business and I'll take care of Mine. Stay focused on the mission. If I need to say something to that man, I'll do it. Don't you worry about it. Do what I've called you to do, and don't forbid others from doing what I've called them to do."

A corollary concern for leaders is keeping individuals and groups within the organization focused on the mission. It is possible to do this and even to sharpen the focus by setting up internal competitive situations. Sales contests, quality-control contests, safety contests, customer satisfaction contests, attendance contests, etc., are all tried-and-true methods of energizing an organization. A leader's responsibility, however, is to monitor these kinds of efforts very closely, to keep the intensity at the right level, and to be sure everyone's focus is on the ultimate overall good of the organization and its mission.

Corporate annals are full of stories detailing how internal competition, both group and individual, got out of hand. The internal battles became so intense as to become unhealthy and detrimental to the overall effort. Any sort of sabotage, whether by word or deed, must be dealt with very severely. It cannot be tolerated.

Jesus demonstrated over and over a resolve to complete His mission. He was focused. This focus extended to making the best possible use of those who could help. His relationship with John the Baptist is the best example of this. A lesser leader could have seen John and his disciples as competitors. Jesus saw them as important adjuncts and continually praised John. He helped His own disciples to see that others doing good things in His name were to be encouraged, not discouraged.

Some churches have a particularly difficult time with this concept. They become so intense about their own programs, their own numbers, and their own parochial interests that they miss being a part of what God is doing all around them. Wise church leaders will not let this happen.

One of the most positive and productive things about the Promise Keepers movement is that, for the most part, churches have not seen it as a threat, but as a very positive program to be co-opted for the benefit of their men, their church, and ultimately for God's kingdom. The same attitude needs to prevail when God is using Young Life to win young people, or Bible Study Fellowship to disciple ladies, or Campus Crusade to reach college students. When leaders focus on God's kingdom and make sure that is the focus of everyone else, good things happen. The same principle applies in every organizational situation.

CHAPTER 42

HOW TO DISPENSE REWARDS

MARK 9:38–41

"I tell you the truth, anyone who gives you a cup of water in my name

because you belong to Christ will certainly not lose his reward."

Mark 9:41

Determining who is to be rewarded and to what extent is, at once, one of the great joys of leadership and one of its most demanding tasks. If you do it well, with discernment, it can be one of the most powerful and effective tools in your leadership arsenal. If you do it poorly, even with the best intentions, it can be a source of consternation, upset, and disunity. The phrase "High risk, high reward" could have been coined to describe the process of determining rewards and allocating compensation. Fortunately, Jesus is a rich source of help and insight for leaders who have rewards to distribute, and everyone does.

Perhaps the first thing to learn about all types of rewards is how important they are. No leader can afford to take them lightly. Wise leaders consider them prayerfully.

The second thing to understand is that money, while usually the most important reward a leader has to dispense, is far from the only one. Leaders who do not understand this are at a significant disadvantage as they deal with compensation issues in their organization. Obviously, monetary rewards had little, if any, part to play in the earthly leadership of Jesus. He rewarded His disciples in other ways—time with Him, unique experiences, great teaching, the privilege of ruling with Him in the kingdom, rich relationships to replace the ones they had lost, sharing with Him in His coming glory, an intimate knowledge of God, and the ultimate gift of eternal life. Some of His rewards were immediate, while many others would be given over time; and the greatest of all His rewards would come not in this earthly life but in the life to come. Jesus offered His followers many rewards which far outweighed the cost of their commitment to Him.

The life and leadership of Jesus teaches us another profound lesson about rewards that goes directly against conventional earthly wisdom. On the surface, it seems naive and counterproductive. On closer examination, it makes ultimate good sense and should form the basis for every leader's reward system.

Conventional wisdom says that to maximize profit, people should be paid as little as possible. Its proponents ask,

"How little can we give this person and still retain and motivate her or him?" Jesus teaches us to ask just the opposite question: "What is the *most* we can afford to give this person and be good stewards of resources and see the enterprise succeed as it should?" Basing our compensation system on the wisdom of Jesus is the most practical and profitable thing we can do. How much, not how little, should be the basic approach to our compensation considerations.

Jesus also teaches us that a static system of compensation will never be best. Some leaders would like to reduce all issues to a cut-and-dried formula. While it is possible to use salary schedules, percentages of profit, and other objective standards, a wise leader will know that no system, no matter how detailed or elaborate, can ever answer all the compensation questions. Again, one reason is that rewards are not all financial or quantifiable in terms of money.

Even where money is concerned, Jesus teaches us that leaders should have latitude in how it is paid. After they meet their obligation to pay what they say they will, wise leaders will be sure they retain enough latitude in how compensation is distributed to make the best use of it. Remember, rewards are not only given for past efforts, but also to motivate and energize toward future success.

Leaders must also learn that the rewards at their disposal are always finite. This means that you cannot give to one person or one group without taking away from another person

or group. This makes all compensation questions more difficult and calls for thoughtful, prayerful leadership.

Even leaders whose compensation pool is made up of
nonmonetary rewards need to understand this. Only one
scholar can be given the top prize. Attention given to one
person in a Sunday school class is attention not available to
others. A pastor's time devoted to one parishioner is time
not available to others. Leaders who understand this and do
their best within this reality succeed and do so with greater
equanimity.

Jesus teaches leaders that "fairness," in the way that the
world understands fairness, is not a totally operable concept
in distributing compensation. In a real sense, He came to do
away with "just rewards." He offers mercy instead of justice.
Even in our small human compensation responsibilities, we
need to move beyond the strict fairness template. As in His
parable of the workers paid equally, Jesus teaches us that
what might seem to be "fair" might not be right or best as far
as compensation is concerned.

To the extent we can, we need to view compensation on
an individual basis through a leadership lens which helps us
to see what is best for each person *and* for the enterprise.
This is not easy, but the best leaders move beyond a simple
formula.

Just as Jesus did, and just as He taught in His parables,
leaders should be able to articulate a rationale for the way
they distribute compensation. When the inevitable question

comes, you should be able to explain why. Your answer may not satisfy the questioner, but it needs to be honest, direct, and defensible in terms of the most good for the enterprise and for the people involved.

Those who cannot accept the rationale might move on. This is okay and should be anticipated. It is not a reason to change the best compensation system which has been thoughtfully and prayerfully considered.

It's also instructive that Jesus here clearly teaches that no good deed will go unrewarded. Even such a tiny thing as a cup of cold water will be noticed by the Lord. Such a "trivial" gesture seems small by the world's standards, but it goes to the heart of what it means to be a servant. Sometimes leaders make the mistake of only rewarding huge accomplishments, the winning of big accounts, the closing of big deals, and so on. But in such a system only the superstars will be rewarded. Wise leaders will also find ways to reward their "cup of cold water" employees.

Rewarding those we lead is a very complex leadership responsibility and privilege. Jesus is the best model to go to for guidance.

CHAPTER 43

THE MILLSTONE WARNING

MARK 9:42–50

"And if anyone causes one of these little ones who believe in me to sin,

it would be better for him to be thrown into the sea with a large millstone

tied around his neck."

Mark 9:42

What is a millstone? It's a huge, heavy circular stone used to grind grain into meal. Usually it was three to four feet across and one foot thick. Donkeys would be attached to the millstone and walk in a circle, slowly grinding the grain. Now imagine attaching such a stone around a person's neck and throwing him in the sea. He would sink to the bottom and suffer a horrible death by drowning. There would be no possibility of escape.

Such a fate would be better than the fate prepared for the man or woman who harms others under their care. Note that the warning is to protect the "little ones who believe in me." This is Jesus' way of protecting the most vulnerable among His followers—the poor, the untaught, the socially disadvantaged, the children, and any other powerless people.

Leaders who accept authority must realize that with authority comes responsibility. Leaders are held responsible for the actions and attitudes of those they lead. They set the moral and spiritual tone for their enterprise. These are among the great prices leaders must pay.

Even with the most godly and consistent leadership at the top, some people may still do bad things. After all, Judas betrayed Jesus after being with Him for three years. Our responsibility as leaders is to be sure that we are not the *cause* of a follower's failure. Part of creating and maintaining the right kind of atmosphere is a zero tolerance for evil within the organization. Many leaders have gotten into trouble by "looking the other way" when knowledge of wrongdoing within their organizations comes to their attention. This *causes* others to consider similar nefarious actions. Never ignore, never cover up, never excuse, and never delay rooting out bad things in your organization. Always deal with them immediately.

Leaders of churches and educational institutions have a particularly awesome responsibility. Strict adherence to Scripture should be a threshold requirement for all those who are entrusted to teach. If a pastor knows that a Sunday school teacher is causing the truth of Scripture to be doubted, or if a college president knows that professors are causing students to question their faith and nothing is done, leader responsibility goes off the charts.

The warning is severe. God will not deal lightly with leaders who abuse or neglect their followers. Better not to be a leader than to hurt those entrusted to your care. This should be a matter of daily prayer.

CHAPTER 44

TAKE UP YOUR AXE

"And if your foot causes you to sin, cut it off. It is better for you to enter

life crippled than to have two feet and be thrown into hell."

Mark 9:45

This verse is, perhaps, the strongest statement on focus in all of the Bible. Jesus is admonishing us all to keep foremost in our thinking the most important goal of every life—to live in intimate fellowship with God. *Anything* which might cause us to miss this goal must be put out of our lives.

Maintaining focus is one of the most important ongoing responsibilities of leadership. It begins with a mission statement and continues as we compare what we are doing and planning with that mission statement. We must be ruthless in discarding those activities and programs which do not contribute directly to the goal as outlined in the mission statement. This sounds easy, but it is not. It is the leader's responsibility to maintain focus.

Consider a Sunday school class which is formed with a very simple mission: to study God's Word. One hour a week is set aside for the sole purpose of Bible study by a homogeneous group. There is a simple mission with a very sharp focus.

Here is what often happens. Someone says it would be nice to open the class with a song or two. Fine. The class begins with singing.

A suggestion is made that the class should promote "fellowship" among its members. Fine. Time is set aside at the beginning of the class for coffee and fellowship. Class time is taken to discuss and plan for fellowship opportunities outside of class. ("Should we have a potluck or a picnic? How does two weeks from Friday fit into everyone's schedule? How about three weeks from Friday?")

The church leaders recognize that many who come to Sunday school do not stay for the worship service so they see class time as perfect to make general announcements. Time is set aside for this.

Since the Bible admonishes us toward good works, the class decides it should support a charitable endeavor. Which one? How much should be given? When can someone bring a report on how our money is being used?

You get the idea. The focus on Bible study, the real purpose of the class, has been lost. Bible study is, at best, relegated to a lesser role; and the goal of a discipled class has been dissipated.

Maintaining focus can be both costly and painful. It won't be easy for that Sunday school class to regain its original vision—especially when those other "worthy" goals have been added. The human tendency is always to drift away from our original commitments. But when we sense that happening, the cost of moving against the tide will be enormous. It's like cutting off a hand or plucking out an eye.

You can't do that kind of surgery without great pain. That is why some churches, colleges, and organizations drift endlessly for years and years, and in the end bear little resemblance to what they once were. No one is willing to get out the axe and start hacking away. But that is precisely what must be done.

By the same token, this passage has a great deal to say about leaders who come into organizations that have drifted and lost their vitality. You'll need many things to revive your company—faith, patience, wisdom, a winsome spirit, a long-term focus, an ability to separate the trivial from the crucial. All those things are needed. But remember what Jesus said. Take a sharp axe with you to work. Sooner or later you're going to need to start chopping away at the things you don't really need. You can't get back on track without it.

Focus is about making sure only the *best* goals are pursued. "Best" must be defined as those goals most consistent with the mission statement. Maintaining focus needs to be an ongoing, daily discipline for leaders.

CHAPTER 45

WORTH YOUR SALT
MARK 9:42–50

"Salt is good, but if it loses its saltiness, how can you make it salty

again? Have salt in yourselves, and be at peace with each other."

Mark 9:50

Both in this passage and in the Sermon on the Mount, Jesus used the salt metaphor very powerfully. Leaders of today, in all kinds of enterprises, need to appropriate this lesson.

In biblical times, salt represented the faithfulness of God. Salt reminded the Israelites of how faithful God had been to them, how He had kept His promises. Today's leaders need to be faithful, to be faithful to their mission, to those they have asked to follow them, and to the standards of godly leadership. Nothing harms an enterprise and those involved in it more than the unfaithfulness of a leader.

As moral absolutes have been leached out of our society, we have seen more and more leaders of business and industry fail the faithfulness test. They have been unfaithful in ways which range from outright stealing to managing the enterprise for their own personal gain rather than accomplishing the mission for the good of all involved. Some have been personally unfaithful in leading lives outside the office which have brought public shame to them, their followers, and the enterprises they have been chosen to lead. Tragically, leaders in and of the church have far too often been unfaithful in exactly the same ways as those with other leadership responsibilities.

Leaders and those who hold them accountable need to understand that they must adhere to a high standard of faithfulness. They need to be able to say to those who follow them, "I have been faithful. I expect the same from you." When a leader cannot make this statement, an essential leadership asset is gone and much of the high ground of leadership has been lost. It is almost impossible to recover.

A line from the great Steve Green song should be the motto for leaders of today: "May those who come behind us find us faithful." It should be a part of our daily prayer to God.

As Jesus spoke about salt, He also had the other metaphorical uses of salt in mind. Salt adds flavor, a tang of excitement to food. What an important lesson! Leaders need to be alert for ways to make their enterprise interesting and exciting for those involved. Leaders need to see that followers do not settle into a dull routine, a kind of "another day at the office" syndrome. When this happens, effectiveness is lost and energy levels go down.

Obviously, the excitement factor is easier to maintain in some enterprises than in others. A major league baseball player has more inherent excitement in his job than a guy making widgets in a factory in Peoria, but a part of every leader's responsibility is to generate excitement for the mission, whatever it is. My dad was in the paint manufacturing business all his life. This might seem to be the epitome of dullness. But because my dad understood the importance of his product in the lives of people, he was passionate about it and made it interesting and exciting to those involved. Every leader needs to be able to make the enterprise's purpose known and meaningful.

Certainly, those who are involved in the work of the church should never be bereft of interest and excitement. Their mission is the most exciting, challenging, and vital of all. The consequences of what is done or not done are paramount and eternal. Excitement and vitality should reign. Sadly, this is often not the case. An attitude of "same old, same old" often prevails. Church leaders cannot, must not, let this happen on their watch.

Leaders in the church need to be excited themselves and to generate excitement in those they lead. Otherwise, such banal considerations as worship style and the next budget campaign become the focal point of the church. Leaders need to focus on the life-changing, destiny-affecting role of the church and display it constantly before all involved. Otherwise, keeping the organizational machinery running becomes the uninspiring goal.

Jesus also taught about the preserving aspect of salt. While demonstrating faithfulness and generating excitement, leaders need to be sure they are working to preserve the things that matter most in their enterprises. This is an admonition of particular importance for leaders coming into a new situation. In an effort to make needed changes and generate new enthusiasm, be wise in preserving the good already there.

As a college student, I had a firsthand experience with a leader who did not understand the necessity of preserving the good things of the past. A new president came to the college full of passion for the job and determined to move the institution forward. In his zeal to do this, he mandated many changes. Some of these were changes in the decades-old traditions of the school, which were precious to students, faculty, and alumni. Enthusiasm for the new president turned to outright rebellion, and he was gone in a very short time. He failed to understand a leader's responsibility to preserve the good things of the past. Do not make this mistake as you lead.

The salt metaphor of Jesus was powerful in His day. It should be just as powerful in the lives of today's leaders. Be faithful. Be excited. Be preserving.

CHAPTER 46

MARRIAGE AND LEADERSHIP

"Therefore what God has joined together, let man not separate."

Mark 10:9

It is no exaggeration to say that we were made for marriage. When all is said and done, and when the final count is taken, most people will be married at some time. Not that marriage is better than singleness. It all depends on the two people who are married and the one person who is single. Many people can best fulfill God's will for their lives by remaining single forever (1 Cor. 7:7–8). Others may choose to marry later in life. But that should not obscure the main point: *Marriage is one of God's best gifts to the human race.* Proverbs 18:22 says, "He who finds a wife finds what is good and receives favor from the Lord." Hebrews 13:4 adds that "Marriage should be honored by all."

The statistics bear this out. Even though the divorce rate is soaring, marriage is more popular than ever before. Consider the following: There are twice as many married men as single men, almost ten times as many married men as divorced men, and twenty-three times as many married men as widowed men. Among both men and women in virtually every age category, those who are divorced and widowed remarry at a higher rate than never-married people do.

What does all this have to do with leadership? Jesus used a question by the Pharisees as an occasion to teach His followers about the sacredness of marriage and the danger of divorce. Marriage was God's idea in the beginning. The notion of one man with one woman for a lifetime goes all the way back to Adam and Eve in the Garden of Eden. God intended that they be joined together in a relationship so strong that it could only be called "one flesh."

By contrast, divorce was man's idea, a product of the hardness of human hearts. Every person who has been through the breakup of a marriage understands what Jesus means. Though there are times when divorce may be necessary because of sinful behavior, it is never painless or easy.

In our day—when divorce has become so common— leaders must do all they can to create a corporate culture in which marriage is upheld and honored. This may pose a problem because our society increasingly has moved away from a biblical viewpoint. In the secular arena, Christians will work side by side with others who may have radically different perspectives on marriage and sexual morality in general. How do you uphold the sanctity of marriage in a pluralistic setting?

The answer is not difficult. Maintain the strength of your own marriage. That means always speaking well of your spouse, making sure that people know you are married, and taking time to nurture your own relationship, even if that means taking some time away from work to be alone together. It also means recognizing the possibility of temptation in the workplace and intentionally setting some "fences" that will protect you from a foolish mistake that could ruin your career and marriage and lead you away from God.

There is a very real sense in which a Christian marriage is a "window in time" through which others catch a glimpse of eternity. We are like actors on a stage with the whole world watching. Our marriage is our starring role. When a husband plays his part well, when a wife plays her part well, the audience sees something deeper; they see Christ and the church. That's the way God set it up, which is why a Christian marriage either draws people to Christ or drives them farther away.

And that is why there is no such thing as a private divorce. If we think it makes no difference if we get a divorce, we are wrong. If we think it is nobody's business but ours, we are wrong. The whole church is involved. God's reputation is at stake.

All around us marriages fail. You hear about it every day. You may work in an office where you are the only person still married to the same man or the same woman. Sometimes you hear about another divorce and you hardly know what to say. People get divorced for the flimsiest reasons.

Here's some exciting news. You are a missionary to that office . . . and your marriage is your message. You don't have to preach a sermon. *Your lifetime commitment to your husband or wife is a visible sermon that people see every day.*

How can you show God's love to others? Let them see it in your marriage. It's more effective than a hundred tracts or two hundred Scripture verses. *People may doubt the things you say, but they cannot deny the reality of a truly Christian marriage.*

Marriage matters to God, and it ought to matter to you. When leaders keep their vows, it becomes easier for followers to keep their promises.

CHAPTER 47

OVERPROTECTING
THE LEADER
———— MARK 10:13–16 ————

People were bringing little children to Jesus to have him touch them,

but the disciples rebuked them.

Mark 10:13

Overprotection is a problem every leader faces eventually. In fact, it's probably true that the more successful you become, the more likely it is that your key people will go out of their way to shield you from unwanted distractions. In the beginning of any dream, leaders will often be found talking with anyone about anything because they aren't encumbered with a staff to manage, a budget to maintain, and a heavy schedule to keep. In the early days leaders *have* to be accessible, if only because they have no one else to talk to and nothing else to do.

Little by little things change. You find a few key people who will join you in your endeavor, you begin to define your goals more precisely, and over time an organization begins to develop around you. You establish procedures, set office hours, and eventually write a policy manual. All of those things are good because they keep you (and your organization) focused on your mission.

However, even the best things in life can sometimes become obstacles. If your policy manual keeps you from seeing people you need to see, then it's time to change the manual.

No doubt the disciples meant well when they tried to keep people from bothering Jesus with their children. One can even imagine them saying, "Look, it's not that Jesus doesn't like children. He *loves* children. It's just that He's busy right now and can't be bothered." That sounds good, and it might have worked until Jesus Himself intervened. Verse 14 tells us that Jesus was indignant. One translation even uses the word *irate*. He interrupted His men, took the children in His arms, put His hands on them, and blessed them.

There are times when a leader must do what only a leader can do. Sometimes you have to cut through the red tape of procedure, even if it means embarrassing your top people in the process. You'll actually create a teachable moment they will never forget.

Take a lesson from Jesus. Don't let anyone "overprotect" you from the people you truly need to see.

CHAPTER 48

THE TRUTH ABOUT FLATTERY

"Why do you call me good?" Jesus answered.

"No one is good—except God alone."

Mark 10:18

Jesus' conversation with the rich young ruler has generated much controversy. The rich young ruler used the term *good teacher* in a rather flippant way (v. 17). Jesus' reply on one level means, "Do you have any idea who you are talking to?" The man evidently saw Jesus as a gifted, Spirit-led rabbi who had unusual insight into the ways of God. But Jesus was not satisfied with that level of understanding. "Don't call Me 'good' unless you know who I really am." Jesus refused flattering comments from people who barely knew Him.

This man was trusting in his own innate goodness to get himself to heaven. He truly thought he had obeyed God's commandments perfectly from childhood (v. 20). Thus, he not only misunderstood who Jesus was; he didn't have a clue who he himself was. He was wrong on both counts—stemming from a defective view of "goodness," which for him was a kind of relative outward morality. He was good by his own moral code but was a sinner by the standards of God's perfection.

Contrary to the assertions of hostile critics and cults, in this passage Jesus is not denying His Deity as the Son of God. Elsewhere in Scripture Jesus clearly asserts Himself as the Son of God, the Messiah. As He answers the rich young ruler, in a subtle way He is trying to lead the man to see the truth of His sonship—and at the same time refusing to accept cheap flattery.

Jesus never varied from His mission. One part of that mission involved making sure people knew who He was and why He came. To that end, Jesus corrected misinformation and always gave God credit and glory.

Leadership by its very nature generates positive comments. The better you do your job, the more praise you receive—and the greater the possibility of being badly misunderstood, and of having flattery turn your head. Some leadership positions need to be sort of glamorized for the enterprise to succeed. Leaders in these kinds of positions need to be especially alert to flattery's seductive nature. To put this admonition in the vernacular, "Don't get sucked in."

Or to use the words of Jesus, which are always better, "Woe to you when all men speak well of you. . . ." (Luke 6:26).

Be aware that flattery is a weapon of the enemy. It can lead to arrogance, and arrogance is deadly.

One of the best weapons leaders have to combat a tendency toward arrogance is to keep in mind a clear picture of Jesus kneeling to wash the feet of His disciples.

CHAPTER 49

LEADING VERSUS MANAGING

They were on their way up to Jerusalem, with Jesus leading the way, and

the disciples were astonished, while those who followed were afraid. Again

he took the Twelve aside and told them what was going to happen to him.

Mark 10:32

Note the timing here. At this point in Mark's Gospel, the die is cast and Jesus knows that He is going to Jerusalem to be crucified. The leaders of the nation have hardened their hearts against Him. Nothing can change the ultimate outcome.

Ever since Peter made his magnificent confession in Mark 8:27–30, Jesus has been dropping hints along the way. He knows what lies ahead and, like any good leader, He begins to let them in on the secret bit by bit. He has waited until now because, frankly, His men couldn't take it any earlier—and they can barely stand to hear it now.

Now that the time has come, Jesus is specific with the bad news. He identifies exactly what will happen, who will do it, and what they will do to Him—spit on Him, flog Him, and kill Him. No doubt this shocked His disciples, but it also gave them enormous confidence because they knew He wasn't caught by surprise in Jerusalem. He walked into that city with His eyes open. He predicted it, and it came true just as He said.

Picking the right time to tell what you know can generate enormous confidence in your followers and give them courage when the hard times come. Even so, the disciples were "astonished" and "afraid." Real leaders often astonish and frighten as they lead. They break new ground, take new territory, and ask for new kinds of commitments. They make new kinds of commitments themselves. Maintaining the *status quo* is what managers do. This is not at all a bad thing, but it is not leadership. Leadership, by its very definition, means being out front blazing new trails. This always causes amazement, fear, and discomfort. The leader is almost always the one who is called upon to give the most.

This passage should call potential leaders to ask themselves some very fundamental questions. The first is: "Am I willing to lead—really lead?" In business, education, and the church, I have seen what happens when people have aspired to leadership positions, attained them, and then refused to lead. When their organizations "were on their way up to Jerusalem," they were not leading the way.

When those who have leadership positions refuse to lead, all kinds of bad things ensue. Decisions aren't made and communicated. Roles aren't defined. Assignments are not made. Discipline is not maintained. Order is not kept, and direction is lost. Their organization never gets "to Jerusalem."

Please do not seek or accept a leadership role unless you are willing to put yourself on the line by making the tough calls and the toughest commitment yourself. Leaders must lead, and it is a difficult and demanding role.

The second question this passage asks potential leaders to consider is: "Am I willing to think of new ways of doing things? Can I think outside the box and color outside the lines? Is it possible for me to astonish some people and even cause fear in others?" As always, Jesus is the example. He was the most revolutionary thinker of all time. He asked His followers then, and asks us today, to think in completely new and different ways. "If it's not broke, don't fix it" is not a motto for leaders. A leader should see every enterprise as "broken" to the extent of asking the questions, "How can it be done better?" and "Are there new and untried ways we can use to improve?" This is what leadership is about. Managers accept things as they are. Leaders do not.

There is a third very important question this passage asks leaders to consider. "Am I willing to be open enough, vulnerable enough, and intimate enough with a core group of followers that I can share bad news with them in a timely way? Will they have learned enough about the mission and my commitment to it to still follow me 'up to Jerusalem' after they have heard it?" Some leaders don't engender enough confidence in their followers to feel they can handle bad news and tough times, so they only dispense good news. This is not the way Jesus led. He continually told His disciples both about the coming kingdom and about the terribly high cost of bringing it about. This is a lesson for all leaders.

As you lead and consider leading, ask yourself the questions this passage evokes.

CHAPTER 50

TOTAL COMMITMENT
MARK 10:35–45

"What do you want me to do for you?" he asked.

Mark 10:36

James and John came to Jesus seeking the ultimate no-cut contract, the quintessential golden parachute. They wanted Jesus to promise them, on the spot, based on what they had done in the past, untold future riches. What they got was a wonderful leadership lesson from Jesus. It is a lesson from which we can all profit.

No matter what kind of group you lead, you will have, or be perceived to have, largesse to distribute. You can be sure that your followers will come to you in the same way that James and John came to Jesus, seeking to make the best possible deal for themselves. By using Jesus' example, you can make the situation profitable for all concerned and, at the same time, move your mission forward.

First of all, Jesus heard them. He listened to them. He didn't say, "Your request is ridiculous. Get outta here." He asked them to go into their request in more detail. In doing so, He learned a lot. He learned something about their opinion of Him and of His power and authority. This told Him a great deal about the two men and about how much they had grasped of what He had been trying to teach them. He had to be pleased with what they had learned, if not with their selfish motive.

If an employee comes to a corporate leader and asks for guaranteed future pay increases, that is one thing. If he comes asking for a guaranteed pay increase based on the profitability of the company, that is something much more in favor of the employee. The request which puts the employee in the most favorable light is the one which asks for a future raise based on the *increased* profitability of the enterprise or the *increase* in its stock price. This signifies that the employee is not trying to renegotiate based on past performance, but is saying, "I believe in this company and am willing to work hard to make it even more profitable. I want to share in its success."

A wise leader will follow the example of Jesus when followers come seeking increases based on past performances, and he will present future challenges to them. James and John came asking for a great deal. Jesus challenged them to earn it by performing through future difficulties. This is a terrific way to handle those who come to you. It provides you with insight about their confidence in the enterprise and in you as a leader. It asks them to increase their commitment. It provides them an incentive to do better for a longer period of time.

Good leaders don't sugarcoat the commitment they seek. Jesus took the brothers' request at face value and challenged them to join Him in an incredible adventure that includes sacrifice beyond anything they have experienced so far.

When Jesus asked, "Can you drink the cup I am drinking?" He was in essence inviting them to come and die with Him. Here we come to the bottom line of life. "Are you willing to sacrifice everything that is dear to you in order to follow Me? If the answer is yes, then you can also share in the rewards."

This has huge implications for leadership. First, you've got to be involved in something worth a total commitment. Second, the leader must himself have made a total commitment. You can't ask people to do what you haven't done yourself. Third, the followers must be challenged to give all they have in the hopes that by united effort, some goal may be accomplished together that could not be accomplished individually.

These are not words to toss around lightly. You only make this kind of challenge when you have found something worth giving your life for.

CHAPTER 51

THE ROYAL ORDER OF SERVANTS

MARK 10:41–45

"Not so with you. Instead, whoever wants to become great among you

must be your servant."

Mark 10:43

Now the disciples have started to argue among themselves, which shouldn't surprise us. The whole episode begins with the strange request of James and John and ends with a heated dispute. It's all perfectly natural because we were born to compete, to fight for the top spot, to look out for number one. Winning and losing is what it's all about. Whether we admit it or not, getting ahead of our friends is a major motivation in everything we do. Before we condemn the disciples, we ought to take a good look in the mirror.

Jesus didn't condemn them. He used their bickering as an occasion to challenge them to channel their ambition in a brand-new direction.

Ambition has become something of a dirty word in our day. To many people it implies an overwhelming desire for personal advancement regardless of the cost—and regardless of who is hurt in the process. Let's face it. There *is* entirely too much of that kind of ambition in the business world. In every company or office you can almost always find a few people who are willing to play fast and loose with the truth if it will help them climb the corporate ladder. They cut corners, they lie on their expense reports, they spread malicious gossip, they abuse their authority, and they know how to stab you in the back and walk away laughing.

Jesus knew all about men and women like that. And He understood that His followers would be tempted to use the same tactics. With four simple words He radically broke with that kind of ambition: "Not so with you." Then He painted an entirely different picture of ambition. "Do you want to be a leader? That's great because the world needs good leaders. Here's what I want you to do. Become a servant. Pick up a towel and start washing dirty feet. Think of yourself as a slave and not as a master."

No doubt the disciples recoiled at the thought of taking the menial role of a servant. After all, these were the geniuses who had just been arguing about who was going to have the seat of honor at the big banquet in the kingdom. The whole point of picking the seat of honor is to have someone else serve you.

"Not so with you." With those four words Jesus turned the values of the world upside down and established a new fraternity—the Royal Order of Servants. Want to join?

True leadership is not a matter of having a title, a position, or an overwhelming personality. *Leadership is first and foremost a matter of the heart.* Who is the leader we need? The one who is a servant. Find the servant, and you've found your leader. He's not the big shot sitting at the head table. He's the one out in the kitchen serving the meal.

CHAPTER 52

TAKE TIME FOR PEOPLE

"What do you want me to do for you?"

Mark 10:51

For days and weeks Jesus has been on a journey toward Jerusalem. He has an appointment with destiny in that city. The storm clouds of angry judgment are gathering on the horizon. He knows what is ahead. Because He is the Son of God, He sees with perfect clarity everything that is about to happen — the plot, the thirty pieces of silver, the traitor's kiss, the late-night arrest, the trials, the false accusations, the scourging, and the crown of thorns. Most of all, He sees the cross clearly and knows that in just a matter of days He will hang there, suspended between heaven and earth.

This is why He came to earth. This is what the Bible means when it says that "his hour" had finally come.

Today He has come to Jericho, His last stop before climbing the hills to meet His fate in Jerusalem. The crowds were large that day as word spread quickly that Jesus of Nazareth was passing through. As they were leaving the city amid much clamor, a blind man began to call out for Jesus. The crowd rebuked him, but the man would not be silent.

When the sound of his voice reached the ears of Jesus, He stopped and called for the man, who came running to meet Him. "What do you want me to do for you?" He asked. The reply was simple: "I want to see." "Go, your faith has healed you," Jesus said. Instantly the man's eyes were opened, and he followed Jesus down the road.

Only one comment is necessary. I don't doubt that Jesus had a lot on His mind. He must have been looking ahead to those final few days in Jerusalem when He would enter as king to the cheers of the crowd, only to be crucified with two thieves five days later. No one could blame Him if He simply didn't have the time to bother with a blind man in Jericho.

But He stopped and took the time to heal him. Ponder that thought for a moment. Everything in this book has testified to the fact that Jesus stands alone among the great figures of world history. No one else can be compared to Him. He is a category of one—the eternal Son of God.

This little story of Jesus and the blind man summarizes everything we've been trying to say about leadership. Leaders are the people who show the way because they have a clear sense of where they are going. They walk into the future with courage and challenge others to follow them. They are often misunderstood and sometimes bitterly opposed. They stay focused on the things that matter, but they never forget that people matter more than things. They fight tenaciously for what they believe in because they believe in a cause bigger than themselves. That cause consumes them and becomes the rallying point for everyone who follows them.

And as this story demonstrates, true leaders take time for people. Let that be the final leadership lesson of Jesus. While you are on your way to the top, keep your eyes open for the people God puts in your path. Almost every day you'll find someone who needs the help only you can give.

This book is now finished, but your adventure of following Jesus—the ultimate Leader—is just beginning.